Praise for Audaciously Alive

"I CAN'T IMAGINE a book where the title more accurately captures its author! Roxanne is both audaciously alive—and one of the most purposeful leaders I have ever met. She is a treasure—and she presents a treasure trove of both insight and practical steps to move you from where you are to where God wants you to be. I loved this book and I know you will too. As her grandfather said, 'She is a 'Sampson!' "

—SCOTT MCKAIN, Author of ICONIC
and a Member of the Professional Speakers Hall of Fame

"A MUST-READ for anyone going through the journey of diagnosis and recovery; knowing there's more to it than accepting a life less than audaciously healthy and full of gratitude for all that the process unfolds."

—JENNY BITNER, Mind, Fitness, and Business Coach

"READING *AUDACIOUSLY ALIVE* felt like a door had been flung wide open and I was given an all-access pass to the journey of a life lived fully alive. Audaciously Alive shows truly how you can overcome by taking inventory of your experiences in life and then take action toward a life fully lived and celebrated. This book will challenge you, inspire you, guide you, and help you value yourself to the degree that you deserve to be valued. One of my favorite parts is the way Roxanne has created takeaway points and questions to help you explore your way to living audaciously alive. I am inspired by Roxanne and grateful for her friendship."

—KELLEY WARREN Augi, Worship Leader, Pastor, Wife and Mom

"ROXANNE'S WORDS impart to us, in a very powerful way, that we were designed to create, listen to our own inner voice, and know intrinsically that we have the power to choose the best every moment. It is a great reminder that we are destined to fully live every day even in the midst of difficult circumstances. I'm thankful that Roxanne draws the detailed picture that God knew what he was doing when he crafted each of us uniquely to be on the specific and wonderful journey that is ours to take. We are audacious and we get to believe it wholeheartedly because that is the plan."

—YETTA DEKKER, Solid Rock Realty Owner and Investment Realtor

audaciously alive

**CHOOSING
TO
LIVE WELL**
on Purpose

Roxanne Harris

Forefront
BOOKS

Published by Forefront Books.
Distributed by Simon & Schuster.

Library of Congress Control Number: 2022910882

ISBN: 978-1-63763-088-4 (Print)
ISBN: 978-1-63763-089-1 (eBook)

Cover Design by Bruce Gore, Gore Studio Inc.
Interior Design by Mary Susan Oleson, BLU Design Concepts

This book is dedicated to all the women who desire to rise above their pain or diagnosis and live life as the passionate, radiant, and audacious women they were created to be.

To my three gorgeous daughters—Ashleigh, Hannah, and Cadence— who are more than enough. May you always live audaciously alive. I love you to the moon and back.

Contents

Part 3: Steps Forward

Introduction

I'VE SPENT most of the past twenty years hiding my pain, loneliness, sadness, anger, and rage. I've viewed myself with disapproving disgust at the way I visually look and move, and I've been doing everything I can to appear "normal" (whatever that is) to the outside world, especially to people of influence or importance.

As a young woman I liked the way I looked and loved that my body was fit and strong. I oozed confidence in everything I did and how I presented myself. I commanded attention when I entered a room, even at a young age. I held my head high and made eye contact with radiance and assuredness.

Somewhere along the way, however, I lost my radiance. I lost my confidence. I lost myself in a sea of physical and emotional pain, unrelenting grief, explosive rage, and shameful bodily disfigurement and disgust. I became obsessed with how I appeared to others as I stood in the glares of those around me. I positioned myself in ways to keep others from seeing my deformities. I did this so I could protect my heart and spirit from their crushing and sometimes savagely hateful comments toward me. I did this so I could protect my children from experiencing the palpable hate that our world has for those who are differently abled.

INTRODUCTION

Many years ago, I was seeing a new client in my clinic. That was nothing unusual since I have multiple new clients every week. This day, however, was different. This day solidified in my mind that I was no longer seen as "normal" in another person's eyes. This day hammered deep into every crevice of my soul that people were judging me based on how I looked, not on who I am.

At the end of the appointment, my new client told me he would never be back. I looked at him puzzled. I thought the appointment had gone quite well and that he had seemed very interested in what I had to say about how he could redirect his health. "It's because of how you look," he said as he sized me up and down. "You obviously know nothing about health," he said, laughing as he went out the door.

How I look? What is that supposed to mean? What does my body fusing my spine together have anything to do with my understanding of health and his digestive problems? I screamed in my head.

At first I was shocked. Then I was crushed. That deep sorrow then turned into rage—rage directed at him, rage directed at my body, rage at the diagnosis, rage at what my life had become, and rage that I had not yet cracked the code to healing myself. That night I bawled—like, ugly cry bawling. I told my husband that people think I am a hideous monster, and I believed it was true. "Look at me!" I screamed. He told me I was exaggerating, and that people don't really think that; and more importantly, he doesn't see that when he looks at me.

I wasn't convinced. "You have to say those things because you are my husband."

"No," he assured, "it's because I do not see any of that when I look at you. I see my beautiful wife, the woman I love."

This would be the first of many incidents of being bullied as an adult, based solely on my outward appearance—the first time I received words that would shatter my confidence, my self-esteem, my self-worth, my perceived value as a person, a woman, a wife, and a mother.

Sticks and stones, I was learning, were way better than name-calling.

In my journey of discovering healing for my body, mind, and spirit, I became more aware of how interconnected all three parts of my body are. I was irritated yet fascinated to discover how an attack against my soul or an emotional standoff could so profoundly affect my physical well-being or how an encounter with the living God could bring such extreme relief to my ravished, pain-stricken body.

The lessons I was confronted with during my pilgrimage toward reimagining and reinventing life inside a body that had been so wrecked with pain, so oppressed, so discouraged, so pitied, so bullied, so outcast, so given up on and left for the plight of a wheelchair, are the lessons that continue to serve me in the beautiful life I have cocreated with God and my husband, Scott (aka, my Mr. Wonderful, more on that later), who never gave up on me and my desire to live life well every day, free of pain and limitation.

I'm not sharing the life lessons I have gleaned along the way as a sad story of struggle and pain but as a story of a woman who rose out of the ashes of debilitating diagnosis, refused to get in a wheelchair, and took control of her life by sheer grit and tenacity with the resolve of reconstructing, recreating, and remodeling what it means to have the audacity to fully engage with my wellness and live well on purpose. Because my life matters. Because this is not a dress rehearsal. Because I want to lay it all down and leave nothing on the table. Because God's promise is abundant life (John 10:10). I want to—and I will—live audaciously *well* every day.

The missing link to living more abundantly is audacity. Audacity is the action behind the thoughts, words, and dreams. It is what transforms dreams into realities. It is the missing puzzle piece that so many struggle to find and so few implement because their reason to live a life of vitality and abundance does not compel them to take massive action.

It is my desire that you will find your own boldness to fight for your life. That out of that boldness you encounter the life God has purposed for you since the moment of your creation. That you will *be* audacious. That you will choose to live life well on purpose, every day, no matter what. Your life is worth living overflowing with vitality and abundance in all areas.

I love you.

May my story inspire you to love yourself enough to be bold, find the warrior within, and create your own beautiful life.

With so much audacity,
Roxanne

PART 1

My Story

CHAPTER 1

Thank God! I'm Not Dying!

"DO I HAVE IT?" I frantically asked the technician, feeling like I would pass out, or vomit, or both. Would he tell me? Could he tell me?

God, please don't let him keep this a secret from me. If he knows, please let him tell me! I need to know!

"What do you think you have?" he quizzed.

"Ankylosing spondylitis," I paused, "that is what they are testing me for, is it not?"

"Yes, you have it," he said firmly without hesitation.

I ran out of the CT scan room and down the hallway as fast as I could to find a pay phone and call home with the good news.

"Hello?" my husband answered.

"I'm going to live!" I blurted out, tears beginning to flow. "I'm not dying!"

"I told you," he said, "all of that stress for nothing."

"Yeah, I'm sorry. I ruined everything. But I'm not dying; I just have ankylosing spondylitis."

"What's that?" he asked.

"I don't know. I just know that I don't have cancer and I am not going to die, that yesterday wasn't my last Christmas with you and the kids!" I said as the tears rolled down my cheeks. The lump in my throat grew bigger as I whispered, "I love you," before I started sobbing and could no longer speak.

Silence on the phone. "I love you too. See you soon," he said.

What a horrible mom, wife, and woman I am to have put my family through that emotional freak-out yesterday. Honestly, Roxanne, get it together. You always imagine the worst and overreact. Scott may not be this forgiving the next time you act this way. Stop being so freaking over-the-top all the time.

Lord Jesus, give me peace. Fill me with Your joy, I prayed as I walked out to my car.

Christmas Day 2000 had been insufferable.

I was miserable the whole day. I couldn't help it. Rather than relish in the day and its memories, all I could think was that this was going to be my last Christmas with my family and that my kids were not going to grow up having a mom. I was grumpy, sad, angry, and downright distraught. I spent the day dreaming up scenarios of next year's Christmas without me. I let my imagination run wild, and I fell further and further into an emotional tailspin that was serving no one, especially not me. The day after Christmas I was scheduled to have a CT scan. The more I thought about the scan and imminent diagnosis, the worse my thoughts were. I had a flair for imagining the most horrific and unrealistic scenarios and convincing myself it was the truth. How many times had I done this before and the result wasn't even in the ballpark of my corrupt imagination? Yet I could not shift my focus. I was completely preoccupied, riddled with fear and anxiety.

I sat there all morning watching my kids opening their presents and imagining them a year from now opening presents without me. I tried to freeze-frame every smile and all their excitement into my memory. Would they miss me? Would they think of me? Would they be sad without me? Would they even care that I was dead? My babies can't grow up without me!

God, please don't let me die. Please let me live long enough for them to graduate high school and see them get married.

Stop it. Stop it. STOP IT! I screamed in my head. *What is wrong with you? You are not dying. Stop saying that. Focus on living today. Tomorrow will have its own problems, and you don't need to worry about them right now. There is nothing you can do anyway. What will worrying accomplish? Nothing! Worrying isn't going to change the diagnosis, but it will rob you of today and this moment. Roxanne, stop being so ridiculous. You are blessed. You are here with them today. Show up for your kids, show up for your husband. Seriously, what is wrong with you? Stop being a downer. Do you really want your kids remembering how sad you were on your last Christmas with them?*

I desperately tried to encourage and coach myself, but this mind game of sabotage and misery continued all day. I simply could not shift my mindset. I was scared to death of what tomorrow's test would bring and what it would mean for our little family.

The day of doom arrived. It was CT scan day. This was back when everything in your medical charts was top secret, and the doctors told you nothing. It was as if you, as the person, were separate from you, as the body. "I'm sorry, Mrs. Harris, we can't disclose that information. It's confidential," they would always say. *Yeah, it's confidential all right*, I would think. *It's confidential about me!* How is something about *me* not allowed to be shared with *me?* This type of logic was a constant source of frustration to me in the early days of the disease.

I was exhausted the morning of the scan after driving the hour into the city for my appointment. I hadn't slept all night, my anxiety was through the roof, and my heart was beating so hard that I thought I would collapse or have a heart attack. My bowels were no help either; they were in rapid evacuation mode as I waited for my impending appointment of doom.

My legs shook as I walked through the hospital trying to find the X-Ray and Imaging Department. I felt physically ill. I seriously considered turning around and running straight out of that hospital, getting in my car, and driving and driving and driving to escape the impending diagnosis. Finally I arrived at the check-in desk, where I was given my file and told to take it down the hall to the X-ray reception desk.

Wait, what? I was holding my file in my hands. I had my file! Now I could see what all the secrets were that the doctors had been writing in my chart for the past six months. I tucked into a doorway like a spy and opened my file, scanning for any information that would help me calm down and answer the questions, *Why was my body in so much pain, and why could I barely walk or move? What did they think I was dying from? What type of cancer did they think I had?*

Then I found it. I saw the words *ankylosing spondylitis* (AS).

What? Well, I sure as heck didn't know what that meant fully, and since it was the year 2000, I didn't own a cell phone, and there was no access to Wi-Fi or Google. But I knew enough from my nursing training and my university medical terminology course to understand that it was something about the spine, and that it wasn't cancer. That was all that mattered to me. I was elated. A wave of relief washed over me momentarily as I exhaled the suffocating fear that had consumed me for months leading up to this appointment.

What I did not realize in that moment was that this diagnosis would become a far greater foe than I ever could have imagined. This disease would rob me of relationships, friends, memories, daily function, sports, sleep, balance, joy, and peace. This inescapable plague would rule my days and mock my nights. All that I would feel and experience second after second, minute after minute, day after day, month after month, year after year would be pain. Pain, pain, and more pain—inescapable, all-consuming pain.

Pain, both physically and emotionally, would be my constant nemesis, driving me toward anger and rage and a seemingly inevitable destruction of my body and soul. Pain would ravish my body and mind and try to kill every semblance of who I was and who I was created to be. Everywhere I went, I was "that woman with AS,"or "that woman who walked funny," or that woman who made others uncomfortable because of the pain that I was in. I was referred to by diagnosis, not by my name. Doctors and friends seemed to forget my name and asked me, "How is your AS?" rather than, "How are you, Roxanne?" Pain, and the focus on it by everyone I knew, was a constant reminder that I was being robbed of experiencing and living my life fully. And there was nothing I could do to escape it—or was there?

My spirit was alive, and God's Spirit was alive in me. God was my superhero, and prayer was my refuge. I grew up with an extraordinary love for God. I had an inner knowing, a feeling, an understanding even as a small child that He was wonderful. I talked to my Daddy, God the Father, all the time. No one taught me to do that. We stopped going to church when I was very young. I have no memories of being in church with my family as a child. What I had was a ceramic plate that hung on the wall in my room until I moved out.

It had a picture of a young child kneeling beside their bed praying before bedtime. It read,

Now I lay me down to sleep,
I pray the Lord my soul to keep.
If I should die before I wake,
I pray the Lord my soul to take.
Amen.

That little prayer brought me great comfort. I prayed that prayer every night with all my might. It made me feel close to God. It gave me assurance that He heard me, that He knew my name, that He would protect me and keep me and those that I prayed for. I knew in every fiber of my being that God answered prayers. I felt a deep connection to God even in my smallness. I believed that He was right there with me every night and believed that anything I asked for would come true. We didn't go to church as a family. I wasn't attending Sunday school. Yet I could feel God calling me to Himself. He was my peace, and He was very real to me.

In the early days of the disease, I spent a lot of time in prayer, not begging for healing or crying for the pain to be taken away. I spent time talking to God about my kids, my hopes and dreams of being there

> *I thanked God every morning for healing me, even though there was no physical evidence.*

for them as they grew. I prayed that I would be a good wife, that my husband and marriage would be blessed. I thanked God every morning for healing me, even though there was no physical evidence. I thanked God for another day on this earth, and I asked Him to help me, to give me strength, to heal me, to set my body free.

I had started praying out of thankfulness and gratitude for being alive rather than begging and pleading with God the way I had done on the day of the scan because my faith and understanding of God had changed over the years. My mindset had changed. The Bible teaches that we don't need to beg God; we can thank Him, knowing that whatever we ask for in the name of Jesus has already been given, expecting good and standing in gratitude and thankfulness rather than envisioning the worst and living in fear.

My prayer life grew as I grew in my relationship with Christ. I became a passionate learner of the Word of God. I became obsessed with prayer and learning more about Holy Spirit. I joined every Bible study and took every course that I possibly could on healing, Jesus, and knowing God. Time spent in prayer shifted my focus away from my problems. I felt overwhelming peace and was full of hope and joy when I spent time with God. If I was having a challenging day or week, my husband would encourage me to go to the healing prayer clinic, saying that I needed it and would feel better after. And I always did.

Jesus became my rock, my place of refuge, my strong tower, my place of safety. With Him I could not just get through the day—I could thrive. Jesus was my bread and my breath. His presence in my days made it possible for me to endure the pain and torment in my body. His presence in my nights made it possible for me to sleep, recharge, and rest in His perfect love.

All I know is that Jesus Christ changed my life for the better, and without Him, I am quite certain I would have died long ago, spiritually, emotionally, and physically, because of the plague of pain.

Lightbulb Moments to Build Audacity

1. Live your best life every day. We are not promised tomorrow. Do not allow fear to steal your day, your week, your month, or your year. Refuse to allow anything other than hope, peace, joy, and love to have a foothold in your mind, your mood, and your relationships.

2. Diagnoses do not define our existence. You are not a disease. You are not a statistic. You are a person of great value and worth. Refuse to be identified or labeled as anything other than your beautiful self.

3. Prayer works. Prayer is a superpower. Prayer quiets the mind and body. Prayer reconnects your spirit with God and shifts the focus off your pain and suffering to the realm of heaven, where we find peace, joy, hope, and great love. Prayer is a fantastic way to reframe and see the situation or circumstance from God's vantage point. And He sees very clearly that you were chosen to live and fulfill your purpose.

Audacious Actions to Live Well on Purpose

1. Wake up and declare out loud, "I choose to live well on purpose today!"

2. Look in the mirror, deep into your eyes, and say, "[your name], you are amazing!"

3. Be grateful for each day. Pray and thank God that you are alive; thank Him for healing you and for the amazing day that you get to be a part of.

I THANK YOU, FATHER, for this amazing day that I get to, and choose to, be a part of. I thank You that You created me with Your own hands while I was yet in my mother's womb and that You made me wonderfully well. I choose to live on purpose today. I choose to be filled with hope, peace, love, and joy and to share what You have given me with the world around me. Thank You for this day to shine my awesomeness on all those whose paths I cross. In Jesus' name, Amen.

CHAPTER 2

I Am Samson

MY GRAMPA called me Samson; it was his special nickname for me because as a child, I was a strong-willed, independent tomboy who just happened to be physically very strong, like Samson in the Bible. My siblings called me Oxanne because I was the extra muscle my dad would call on when he needed help; I was "strong like an ox."

I loved my Grampa and he loved me. He was the kindest, most fun-loving, and gentlest person I knew. I will never forget the day he walked in our door after work and asked the question he always asked, "What's for dinner? Jellybeans?" We all started to giggle because we knew the surprise that was waiting for him on his dinner plate. Grampa sat down and lifted the pot lid off his dinner plate to find a mountain of jellybeans underneath! He roared with laughter and started eating them, sharing them

We get to choose how we show up every day and in every situation.

with all of us. Grampa was not afraid to laugh, cry, or enjoy life. I wish I had paid more attention to his zest for life and asked him while he was still here with us why he lived with such peace and joy. Grampa used humor to turn the mundane or stressful moments into joyous ones. This is an important concept to remember for those living with chronic pain: we get to choose how we show up every day and in every situation. Mindset is everything. We make or break our days by our reactions and responses.

In tenth grade, my gym class went to the school's workout room. The boys were all showing off. One of the macho boys was doing leg presses, and all the guys were in awe as he pressed 200 pounds. I was a lean, mean muscle machine because of my athleticism and dance training, and I was also very competitive, always pushing myself to outdo my best performance and outperform those around me. I always had the drive to be the best and to show what I was made of. I couldn't be shown up by a boy, so I said I could probably press 220 pounds. Everyone laughed. After all, I was a 5'8½" tall girl who weighed 112 pounds, and I had never been to a gym before. They set up the weights for me and I sat down on the bench. With very little effort I slammed the press forward and all their mouths fell on the ground. It was so easy! Perhaps it was my natural strength, but more likely my grit to prove myself that pushed me to success. I was often teased due to the size of my thighs.

I was sometimes called *thunder thighs* because my quads and hamstrings were ripped. I was proud of my body, my muscles, my strength, and my ease of movement. I earned a lot of respect that day, and I proved that my thighs were for more than just looks. I felt like Wonder Woman.

Wonder Woman had long inspired me, and I felt that I was like her in many ways. I tried to model her tenacity, passion, and strength of mind and body. She fueled my desire to find a way and make it happen, no matter what.

The Accident

I was sixteen and had spent the summer helping in the kitchen of the restaurant where I worked. The men who worked there were much taller than I was and stacked sixty-pound crates of chicken way above my head, right up to the ceiling of the walk-in refrigerator. One day I went to grab a crate of chicken to prepare for the supper rush. I was in a hurry, and rather than try to find someone to help me, I decided I would reach up above my head and grab one of those crates by myself to save time.

As I brought down the crate, its weight and the force of the drop were more than I could handle. I twisted to the side to find a safe place for it to land that was not the top of my head or my feet. I felt the full weight of that crate pop something in the middle of my back, causing piercing pain that sent electric shocks up and down my spine, taking my breath away. I did what I always did: I sucked up the pain and kept working because I was Samson, and big girls don't cry. I didn't have time for pain. I had to get my work done because I had a hot date that night with my boyfriend (now my husband), and we were going bowling.

I finished work, noticing that my back was getting more painful. I thought there was not much that I could do about it and went bowling anyway. When I got out of the car, I felt a very weird pain in my hip but said nothing. With the first throw of the bowling ball, I felt excruciating pain in my back, hip, and down my whole right side. I felt something shift, slide, and lock in my pelvis. I was frozen. I could not unlock my hip and stand up. I was half-cocked to the side, locked in place like a statue on a bowling trophy, frozen in pain.

What on earth had just happened? My body screamed for help, but my brain said, *Whatever you do, do not show weakness. Do not show anyone that you are in pain. Get up, act normal, be normal. You are not a sissy. Be cool.* Being cool didn't last long. I went to the emergency room a few days later. The doctor said it was nothing more than a strain and prescribed a painkiller. I went back a few weeks later in more pain than before, and he prescribed physiotherapy, again asserting that there was nothing seriously wrong and nothing he could do other than prescribe more painkillers.

I went to physiotherapy three times a week, but the pain got worse, not better. Months went by with no improvement. It got so bad that I was not able to get off the treatment table at the end of my session because my back would go into spasms.

I was sixteen years old, and I limped around in constant pain. After months of intense therapy, the physiotherapist called my doctor telling him that she thought I had sprained my back and had a herniated disk.

I went for X-rays, and my doctor told me again that there was nothing he could do but that he would refer me to a specialist to see if they could help me surgically. I limped around for two years in constant pain until one night my dad noticed that something was wrong.

I shared a room and a bunk bed with my sister. One night as I was getting ready for bed, I threw my leg up onto the top bunk as I did every night (because I was too old and too cool to use the ladder), and when I did, my hip and back locked into place and I couldn't move. I was stuck in mid-air, screaming in pain. My dad heard me and came into my room yelling at me, demanding to know what was going on. He grabbed me and yanked me down off the bunk bed. Through my tears and pain, I told my dad that I had been in constant pain, going to physiotherapy and taking medication for over two years. He was angry and demanded to know why he was never told this, but more importantly he wanted to know why I was taking prescription painkillers instead of getting the problem fixed.

The next day my dad set up an appointment for me with his chiropractor. My mom, who had been a nurse, didn't believe in chiropractors and said they were quacks. She didn't think this would help me, but my dad had used chiropractic for years and was convinced this was the only thing that would help me.

It was the strangest experience. Dr. Geoff asked me a few

questions and had me stand on one leg, then the other. He had me lie on a table with a hinge in the bed that allowed the table to drop down, which I thought was strange, until he slammed my lower back with such force that I knew exactly the reason for that hinge. In shock and hardly able to breathe from the adjustment, he told me to get up and stand straight. I was surprised to get up and not feel any pain or twinges in my back at all. He told me to walk around, and amazingly, I wasn't limping! I wanted to hug him. Finally, after two years and just one chiropractic adjustment, I could walk pain-free! All the pain had vanished. I was in awe. Dr. Geoff told me that I needed to come back to get everything else aligned, and I was happy to do so. He had sold me on chiropractic. My dad looked very pleased with himself. When we got home, I told my mom what had happened and showed her how well I was walking. She could not believe what she was seeing. "Impossible," she said. But that particular "impossible" was possible for me. Sometimes our breakthroughs come from the least-expected places.

My dad was not our family's doctor. He was anti-sickness, and according to him, every illness, ache, or pain was always in our head. He believed in nature's medicine: food. There is a scripture that says, "As a man thinks, so is he." (This is a common paraphrase of Proverbs 23:7.) I never knew my dad to be a man of faith outwardly, but he did believe that anything could be overcome with the right mindset. My dad opened the door to the realm of natural solutions for me. Regardless of my mom's fierce opposition and criticism of chiropractic, it worked for me. That experience showed me that there was always another option. I didn't need surgery or medication; I needed an adjustment.

By the time I saw the specialist, he couldn't find anything that required surgery. I explained what had happened with Dr. Geoff and how he gave me back my life. The specialist scoffed and told me that chiropractors were quacks. He referred me to a sports medicine clinic for ongoing physiotherapy to strengthen my back and told me to stop wasting my time with Dr. Geoff. As a nursing student, I respected his opinion and started back with the physiotherapy. Not surprisingly, within a couple of months, I was back at Dr. Geoff's getting the treatment that really worked for me.

Sometimes we must look outside of the box for solutions to our pain, even if that means trying something that is considered fringe. If the treatment is working and you are getting results, why would you stop just because someone else isn't open to other possibilities?

Our treatment strategies need to be individualized and in line with our vision for our health.

We can become so cemented in what we think we know that we can shut down alternative options altogether.

If your doctor doesn't understand natural treatments, it doesn't mean they don't work; it just means the doctor needs to do more research. Medicine is not a one-size-fits-all approach. We should expect to be treated as an individual, not as a number. Our treatment strategies need to be individualized and in line with our vision for our health. My wellness goal at that time was simple: I wanted to enjoy life without pain.

Lightbulb Moments to Build Audacity

1. You are not a sissy. Asking for help is not weak. You can get help and still be Samson. Reaching out and asking for help when you need it is a superpower.

2. Natural solutions work. You may have to try many modalities and therapies or combinations of therapies for optimal success.

3. When you find a treatment that works for you, stick with it no matter what. Some therapies will work for a season and then you may have to try something else. Healing is a process, and the body heals on different levels over time. Listen to what your body needs and be flexible in your wellness protocol to make the changes that support or increase the benefits and results of your healing journey.

Audacious Actions to Live Well on Purpose

1. What mindset do you need to achieve your wellness goals? Journal where you need to have more tenacity with your health decisions.

2. Choose to live well regardless of how you feel. Make a firm choice to live well on purpose. Start today to find the health freedom you seek.

3. Be open to natural solutions. A wellness journey often requires a team approach. If you need the support of multiple healthcare providers, ask for recommendations and arrange a meet-and-greet to interview the practitioners to see if they are a good fit for you and your wellness journey.

CHAPTER 3

Mama Bear

WE MOVED across Canada for Scott's job promotion at the end of August 1998. We had come to the area the month before on a house-hunting trip and had left our three young daughters with my sister for the week, knowing they would enjoy spending time with their cousins.

The day we arrived in Ontario, I felt something was wrong back home. I tried calling my sister's home that evening, but there was no answer. So I called my mom, thinking that they may be visiting with Gramma and Grampa. Sure enough, all the kids were there on a sleepover. My sister had been stung by a wasp and was in the hospital with an anaphylactic reaction, leaving Gramma and Grampa to babysit all six grandchildren for the next few days.

When I spoke with my oldest daughter, who was just

shy of five at the time, she told me that one of her uncles was not being very nice to her. My fourteen-year-old brother, who was a class clown, was usually unaware when he was being too rough for his nieces and nephews. She told me that she had told Gramma what happened, and that Gramma had given him trouble and made him apologize. We talked some more, and she said he was being mean to all the kids so I told her to make sure she told Gramma if it happened again and to tell him to go away and not bother her. My mom confirmed that she had dealt with the roughhousing and that everything was fine, that it was no big deal. My daughter told me that she was okay, yet something didn't feel right.

I hung up the phone feeling angry that my daughter was having a tough time. I wanted to go home immediately. But Scott protested, saying the kids were fine and this was not only a house-hunting trip but also a mini vacation for us. He was right; we had not had a vacation alone since we had been married five years and three kids ago. I tried to shake off the uneasy feeling I had and enjoy my evening with my husband, but I found myself drifting back to that conversation with my daughter. I just felt that something was not right.

A month later we packed up our entire house and moved across Canada. It was exciting. Moving so far away from family and friends was a great new adventure for our little family. Two months later, I was sitting at the dining room table sewing a princess costume for my oldest daughter for her school Halloween parade. It was the only thing in the entire world she wanted to be, a beautiful princess. She had just come home from kindergarten and the other kids were still napping. My mother-in-law was in town visiting, and she was snoring on the couch a few feet away from me.

Out of the blue my daughter came up to me and casually told me her uncle had inappropriately touched her when she was at Gramma's house. The silence was deafening. In that moment, the world stood still and began engulfing me, suffocating the very breath out of my lungs and stealing my last heartbeat. I was in shock. My heart flooded with crushing agony and disbelief. My worst nightmare was alive. My mother-in-law shot straight up on the couch and was suddenly wide awake, pie-eyed and listening to every word.

"What did you say?" I asked my daughter, trying to remain calm. My five-year-old daughter repeated the devastating words verbatim, describing the very actions I had spent my whole motherhood trying to prevent. My entire existence as a woman and mom had been and always will be dedicated to the protection and safety of my children. As matter-of-factly and as calmly as she would have told me about anything that had happened in her day, she told me exactly what she had experienced. She had no understanding for this ordeal. This was not something we had ever spoken about in our home, yet instinctively she knew it was not right. It made her uncomfortable, and rightly so. I was devastated. I was horrified. I was sickened.

I was totally, completely distraught to the very core of my being. My precious baby girl! How could this be happening? I had done everything I could to protect her. I had carefully planned for my daughters to stay with my sister so that my girls would be safe because we had a suspicion that my brother was having some challenges. Shame set in rapidly. Not only did I know, but my mother-in-law had clearly heard the entire conversation and sat there staring at me, speechless. *God, why is this happening?* The very night that I had spoken to my little girl was when this had happened—the very first night we were away. My mama bear senses had been right; I just knew something was not okay. I hugged her and told her I loved her and that I would make it better.

I went to my bedroom, closed the door, and called Scott. Then I lost my mind. I screamed. I yelled. I bawled. I cried all the tears and then some. I wailed until nothing more came out. Hollow, soundless sobs from the depths of my soul. Then my sobs changed as I began vibrating with raw, primal rage. I saw red. It was good that this brother was now thousands of miles away from us because I wanted to rip him to shreds.

Eventually I came out from my room and took my daughter aside to ask more about what had happened at Gramma's house. It became clear that he had wrongly touched some of the other kids as well, so I approached my second daughter who was playing in her room and asked her if anything strange had happened when she was at Gramma and Grampa's in the summertime. Putting down her Barbies, she said *yes* and told me all about how her uncle had inappropriately touched her, how mad she got at him, and how she had told him to stop it and say he was sorry to her. She said he had apologized, and Gramma had told him to not do that again. She was proud of herself for telling on him and said that he didn't do it again. She went back to playing with her Barbies without skipping a beat.

I was not prepared to speak to my daughters about this. I didn't know what to say. I had not read about sexual molestation in any parenting book that I had. I wasn't prepared for this at all. I hoped and prayed that because they were so young and because it was dealt with quickly, they would be able to let it go, if they hadn't already.

When I called my mom, there was no hello, no preamble, no explanation or recall of events. "You knew. You knew and you didn't tell me," I spurted out.

"He's my son. I have to protect him," she said immediately.

"What about me and my daughters? Don't you care about us?" I screamed at her. It was quiet for a long time. The silence was deafening. Eventually my mom spoke.

"He's my son," she said. With that, our conversation was over. There was no offer of support, comfort, or remorse.

We Went Through the Trauma Alone

All my siblings, except one, disowned me. They said if this got out into their community, it would make their lives difficult. One of my siblings even told me my kids were liars, and that I had coaxed them into saying these things. I was abandoned by my own family in my time of greatest need. Since we had just moved across the country, we had no support network. I had made a few friends at church, but I had known these ladies for only two months, and this was not something I wanted to share with people I hardly knew.

The authorities were not helpful at all. They wanted to send someone to my home to investigate to determine if my kids were safe. They couldn't seem to understand that this abuse had happened thousands of miles away, that my daughters were not in any danger, and they would not be seeing this person again. The city police in our community somehow could not talk with the federal police force that had authority in the town where my brother lived. It was complicated and stressful. Eventually an agreement was reached between the two police forces for my brother to have several counseling sessions.

There was never an apology, never any retribution. Nothing in his life changed. Yet everything in ours had. My daughters remember what happened to them. My oldest daughter went to play therapy as a child, and my other daughter started counseling when she was a teen due to anxiety and nightmares she was having about the abuse. Those events left scars in their minds, and they are still learning strategies to help them deal with the anxiety and feelings of those abhorrent actions.

After seven years of minimal communication with my family, we started to rebuild our relationships. Some relationships will never be the same. They will be different, and that is okay. I have come to terms with the fact that not everyone chooses to grow and heal. Not everyone can come to terms with the trauma they caused or contributed to. Everyone tries to forget, but not everyone chooses to forgive. Forgetting without forgiving is like locking yourself in a prison, holding on to the key, and saying you can't get out.

When a situation haunts you, it affects you subconsciously and consciously, affecting your relationship with yourself and those around you, even weighing in on your decision-making process in other areas of your life. It is challenging to trust when the trust has been shattered so completely. I have forgiven my brother. I have forgiven him, but there will not be any relationship between us. With his denial of the events, he drew a line in the sand. A line that cannot be erased by the winds of time, but by remorse alone.

Forgetting without forgiving is like locking yourself in a prison, holding on to the key, and saying you can't get out.

The stress of the abuse was a lot for our family to handle. It drove a wedge between me and my husband. We had not been intimate since we learned what had happened to our girls; it was the furthest thing from our minds. It was as if sex were repulsive altogether. The thought of intimacy would bring up nightmares in our minds of what had happened to our girls. One night we finally reconnected intimately. The moon was shining brightly through the window, illuminating us and the whole room. I could see the love in my groom's eyes—his tenderness, his strength. I felt safe in his arms. I had tears rolling down my cheeks because it was such a beautiful moment, and it felt so good to be held and comforted by him. Spontaneously, out of the depths of my very being, from the chasm of my shattered soul, I silently cried out to God.

God, please give me a child that is untouched. I knew immediately that God had answered my cry and opened my womb to receive life. It seemed impossible, but I knew it was true. I felt life spark inside of me. I didn't say anything to my husband. This was a secret between God and me. A few weeks later on Christmas Day, I woke up and looked in the mirror. It was as if

My son was a miracle— a miracle proving God's goodness, mercy, and love.

there were a neon light on my forehead flashing *Pregnant.* I thought it was crazy since my husband had had a vasectomy nearly two years before that; yet I had prayed for this child and felt like God had answered my prayer. On New Years Eve I took a pregnancy test, and it was positive immediately.

My beautiful son was conceived out of the cry of my heart. I prayed for him, and God answered. My son was a miracle—a miracle proving God's goodness, mercy, and love. I was so excited to see my little miracle. Nine months later, my beautiful son was born.

Lightbulb Moments to Build Audacity

1. Trust your mama bear instincts.

2. Stay connected to your spouse during challenging times.

3. Rebuild family relationships as part of your healing journey.

Audacious Actions to Live Well on Purpose

1. Plan a family or friend reunion to reconnect and build your support network.

2. Find a cognitive behavioral therapist or counselor in your area to work through traumatic events you still dwell on.

3. Write a letter to someone who hurt you in the past, let all your feelings and emotions out, and burn the letter. Put on some appropriate music and stomp out your emotions until you have released everything. Or you could beat a garbage can with a bat or a broom.

CHAPTER 4

There Is No Way in Hell! Life with Chronic Pain

"MOMMY'S COMING," I cried, "Mommy's coming." I clenched my teeth in sheer grit trying to get to my two-week-old son, who was awake and crying across the hall. The pain was astronomical. I could not walk without feeling the agony of sharp, shooting, stabbing, throbbing, recoiling waves of pain everywhere in my body. Nowhere on my body was untouched—my feet, my hips, my back, my neck. Every step was like a scene from the apocalypse. What was happening? Why did my pelvis feel dislocated? Why could I not walk properly? "Mommy's coming," I cried again, trying to hide the sound of fear in my voice. I grabbed onto the walls, the footboard, the door, anything I could use to drag my body across the hall and into my newborn son's room.

It was twelve steps from my bed to his crib, and I could not get there. Every step took for-ev-er. It felt like an eternity simply to cross the hallway to get to my son. I had never let any of my other three babies cry this long. *I am a horrible mom*, I thought. *I am traumatizing my son. He is going to think that I have abandoned him.* These negative, self-defeating thoughts kept coming, slaughtering my heart and mind with feelings of inadequacy, despair, and anguish as I listened to his cries, feeling totally helpless. "Mommy's coming," I cried out to him again. Who could help me? There was no one. No one would even hear me if I screamed for help.

My husband was at work, and my three daughters were not even old enough to hold the baby on their own, never mind get him out of his crib. We lived thousands of miles away from our family on an acre of land. And here I was, not able to walk. My body was not listening to me. It was not working. The pain was insufferable, overwhelming, excruciating. I was desperate to get to my crying baby.

Finally, in total anguish, with sheer force and determination I grabbed hold of his crib and dragged myself along the rail, only to realize I could not pick him up. I could not carry him. I tried to bend over to pick him up, but the pain paralyzed me. I could not breathe. I could not stand up, I was locked hanging over him, feeling like my body was going to collapse. *Lord Jesus, help me. Lord Jesus, please let me pick up my baby.* My mama bear instinct kicked into full gear, and my inner

Samson rose up with the fortitude of sheer will in every cell of my being. By God's grace I picked up my son and made it back to my bed to nurse him.

A few days later I found myself driving into the city to a chiropractor that a neighbor had recommended to me. I lay on the table with hot, wet heating pads on my back for twenty minutes. Then the chiropractor gave me a twenty-minute massage, looked at me, and said, "I can't adjust you. Go home and come back tomorrow. You are too tight." She did not charge me for her services. This scenario was repeated for three days. On the third day, after the heating pads and massage were finished, Dr. Linda gave me a few small adjustments and then had me stand and lift my legs and arms one at a time while pressing on my hips and pelvis. She did this for quite some time. At last, she said something that would forever change the course of my life.

"Roxanne, I don't exactly know what is wrong with you, but there is something terribly wrong. You need a doctor. I am going to write down several tests I would like your doctor to do, but you need to know that there is something very, very wrong and it requires further investigation, more than what I can do for you. I don't want to touch you until we know what is going on." Out of extreme compassion and concern, this beautiful chiropractor, whom I had just met, knew there was something seriously wrong with my body. She wasted no time launching an investigation that would throw me into the world of autoimmune disease, debilitating pain, chronic fatigue, emotional instability, and eventually, a path back to freedom and regaining my life. Dr. Linda cared about me, and that was huge.

People often ask me why I didn't just go to a doctor to begin with. Because I had suffered for over two years after my back injury until a chiropractor got me walking pain-free again, I had honestly never thought once about going to a doctor. It never crossed my mind. Since the day Dr. Geoff first helped me, whenever I had issues with my back or hips, I went to the chiropractor, so in this totally bizarre situation, I felt I needed the help of a chiropractor.

True Compassion in Pain Is Rare

When I saw my family doctor, she readily agreed to all the blood tests, as what I was experiencing was very abnormal and she was genuinely concerned. I will never forget the call I got at 7:10 a.m. I had just woken up and was in the kitchen preparing breakfast for my kids when the phone rang. You know the feeling you get in your gut when you just know that it is not good? Instantly, I knew it was my doctor calling and that something was wrong. This was before the days of caller ID, so it truly was a deep or intuitive sense of knowing.

She explained that she had results of my blood tests and that something was very wrong. The inflammatory markers were extremely high, and my body was behaving like the body of an eighty-six-year-old. We needed to bring down the inflammation as quickly as possible and figure out what was happening. She had already put in an urgent referral to a rheumatologist.

The next few months were a total blur. I got in to see the specialist quite quickly, and more blood tests were ordered along with a battery of X-rays of every joint in my body. It took forever and was so painful. There was no compassion from the X-ray technician as she manipulated my inflamed, stiff body into Cirque du Soleil contortions to get the right images; so much so, that after the series of X-rays, I couldn't get off the table. The pain was astronomical. I had searing pain for days, leaving me discouraged and without relief. That's when I began to realize I was just a number in the system. I was not seen as a real person; I was the woman with uncontrolled inflammation. I was not Roxanne.

I was not treated with care or compassion in most, if not all, encounters that I would have with the healthcare system. I left appointment after appointment, test after test, feeling defeated, deflated, and worse than when I went in. No one encouraged me or checked in to see how I was feeling emotionally. No one asked me how I was coping or whether I was coping at all. I was a number, an object to study, not a person to relate to, connect with, or support. I felt all alone. My friends did not understand my pain or extreme fatigue. We were estranged from my family. I had four kids under the age of five who needed to be cared for. It was just me and my wonderful husband.

Not only was I struggling with everything that was going on physically, but I had also suddenly developed an extreme panic disorder. It was so bad that everything would go black and I would start to tunnel out (start to lose consciousness). I could not speak or move; it was as if I had become frozen in time. Those panic episodes were happening daily, and they were really starting to impede my ability to get anything done, especially outside the house.

The panic attacks were a recent development. Just after my body went crazy with pain when my son was two weeks old, my mother decided she wanted to fly out to meet her new grandson and see her granddaughters. I did not want her to come. I wanted to protect my girls, and I did not want her coming and potentially bringing up bad memories for them. But there was no stopping her. She apologized for not being there for me and wanted to try and work things out. Reluctantly, I agreed to let her come for a visit.

The day my mom arrived, I felt good until that night. All night I felt excruciating pain in my chest. I could not breathe and thought I was going to die. I tunneled out a few times and watched the room spin and go dark. This happened all night long. The next morning, I still felt this way, so I went to the emergency room. After hooking me up to heart monitors and taking some blood, the doctor diagnosed me with extreme panic attacks and sent me home with medication. Eventually I started having full-blown panic attacks in situations that were not even stressful. I would get groceries and not have a panic attack in the store, but after I loaded the groceries into the car and got ready to drive home, I would have an over-the-top panic attack right there in the parking lot to "celebrate" the fact that I did not have one in the store! My emotions were a train wreck. There was nothing I could do to prevent the panic attacks, nothing I could do to get out of them. I was stuck in a crazy cycle, always wondering if I would wake up on the floor somewhere.

When the rheumatologist ordered all those X-rays, I anxiously fixated on all the possible outcomes. The X-rays themselves did not bother me; it was the fear of the unknown. It was what they were going to reveal and if and how I would be able to handle the results. That was what I was freaking out about. Just the thought of going for any type of test caused extreme panic for days leading up to and following the appointment, until I knew the results. In those moments of anxiety and full-on freak-out, I took everyone and everything down with me into my pit of deep despair and the fear that I was going to be told I was dying. I was miserable, my husband was miserable, and my kids were grumpy. We were all unhappy because I had no filter and could not contain my extreme angst of what was to come.

Looking back I realize that my emotional state played a huge role in the level of physical pain I was experiencing. The more fearful and upset we are, the more the body locks down

The more fearful and upset we are, the more the body locks down in self-protection mode.

in self-protection mode. This locking down is also referred to as "holding on for dear life." The more we squeeze and the longer we squeeze, the more our muscles and tendons contract and spasm. I was absolutely holding on for dear life. I had no idea what was happening to my body physically or why I was now freaking out emotionally too. All I could do was hold on and not let go.

The rheumatologist, Dr. Stacey, was concerned about the results of the X-rays and said that I would have to have a CT scan in order to get a definitive diagnosis. This was now the summer of 2000. While waiting for an appointment for the scan, I was started on a cocktail of medications to try to bring down the inflammatory markers. Nothing seemed to be working.

The CT scan happened on December 26, 2000. That was day I learned I was being plagued by a disease called ankylosing spondylitis. Dr. Stacey was happy that we now had a diagnosis to work with, which would guide my treatments, or more aptly, my drug therapy. "Treatments" would assume that I was being treated to be brought back to a state of well-being. In the current medical model, there is no such thing as a return to a state of health for autoimmune disease. It is all about symptom management, mostly through drug therapy. Other than a handout of daily exercises, I was told nothing about how I could help myself to decrease the pain and inflammation. This was before the days of Google and Internet self-help. There was no discussion of which foods to eat or avoid, how to sleep, or how to decrease my stress. It was all about the pharmaceuticals, what drugs they could give me to shut me up and stop complaining about the pain. I tried myriad pharmaceutical drugs. I was put on combinations of medications that caused the pharmacist alarm. He told me many times that I couldn't take these medications at the same time, that they could kill me. As stressful as that was to hear, all I wanted was for the incessant pain to go away. Medication was the only option my doctor had.

Monthly blood tests made sure that my liver was still functioning due to the toxic nature of the medications. I became paranoid about the blood work because of the old battle-ax who worked in the lab. She was a tough old woman who was aggressive and mean. I always left with a bruise the size of a softball. Despite having a working diagnosis and all the various medications, nothing was changing. I was getting worse and feeling less beautiful by the day.

Shoes in the Oven

It's funny how we can self-define beauty. Shoes are such a trivial thing, yet every woman knows that the right shoes complete the outfit. A shoe can make you feel adventurous, flirty, athletic, and even downright sexy. I mostly wear the same shoes day after day, and I am totally fine with it. But there comes a day when I want to wear a high-heeled stiletto on a hot date with my husband to feel sexy, or a knee-high, leather high-heeled stiletto boot for an important meeting where I want to feel powerful and a wee bit flirty. At the age of thirty-three, the arthritis society started to send a physiotherapist to my home. I had major walking challenges by that time.

The physiotherapist made orthotics in my oven and brought metal braces for my wrists and hands so that I could write and hold things. I could not take two steps without wearing these gawdawful sandals spring, summer, autumn, and winter. All I could wear were these hideous therapeutic sandals that helped me to walk without pain. I was a mess, and I was losing my femininity. Who wants to get all dressed up to go to a nice dinner party or event and wear hideous shoes? But that was my new life: a skirt, wool socks, and hideous sandals in the dead of winter. Before it happened to me, I didn't realize how much shoes could mess with a woman's pride, ego, and confidence. The shoes were just another small reminder that I was no longer in control of my own body.

I felt sorry for Scott. He had not signed up for this. It was not just about the shoes. I am certain he did not care what kind of shoes I was wearing out to dinner. It was all the other stuff—the pain, the hobbling around, the untidy house, the myriad doctors' appointments. When I would say to him that I was sorry, that he did not sign up for this life, he always reminded me of our wedding vows and how he meant it when he said "in sickness and in health." He would quickly ask me if he were the one who was sick, would I turn my back on him? Of course not, I would declare. He would always reassure me that the same was true for him.

"I am in this, Roxanne; you can't make me go away. I will always love you and be here for you."

My Husband Is My Mr. Wonderful

No complaining, no negative or condescending comments. Just love. The love of my life, my Mr. Wonderful, would pick up the slack, take the kids to the park or the museum by himself, and take over making dinner when he came home if he saw me struggling. Whispering in my ear, he would tell me to go and lie down while he finished making dinner. He did the laundry, played with the kids, and even weeded my gardens after work, when he didn't want to, because we were in this together, in sickness and in health, till death do us part. Scott was always there for me. I did not need to ask; he could just feel my pain and exhaustion. We never spoke about how much pain I was in—not once. He just knew, and he showed up. Not once did he get upset at me for not doing something.

It is important to know that I always tried my best to be the wife and mother I wanted to be, that I demanded myself to be, every day. I did not lie around. I did not make excuses. Even during the worst possible pain, when every step taken through gritted teeth seemed like it took hours, I got up. I showered. I made my kids breakfast and lunch. I got my kids ready. I took my kids to school and picked them up. Every day. I just did it. I forced myself to do it. I refused to lie down and give up. Giving up was not in my nature. I was Samson, and I would find a way.

We must resist the temptation to crawl into bed and pull the covers over our head as a coping mechanism. Isolating ourselves and refusing to engage with our life does nothing to help the situation. It only adds to the pain and intensifies the limitations on our life. When we do not move it, we lose it. Lying around immobilized was not how I wanted to live my life. I needed to do everything I could to remain as functional and as normal as possible. Showing up for my kids every day was one of those necessities.

Doing my hair and my makeup was another. I didn't want my husband coming home every day and seeing me as a wreck. I wanted him to see his beautiful wife, not the ruins of disease. Even though it was challenging to hold the blow dryer and style my hair, it made me feel good. Bad hair days are the worst, so I make a point of avoiding them as much as possible.

One day, four years into the diagnosis, I went to my regular appointment with Dr. Stacey, and she told me about a new medication that was having spectacular results. She wanted me to start taking it immediately because I had virtually no improvement since the diagnosis. I readily agreed because, quite frankly, living was hard. Breathing was hard. The pain sucked everything out of me before the day even got started. Life was a constant struggle physically, emotionally, relationally, and sexually.

To my surprise, this wonder drug changed my life after just the first dose. I had no pain. I could walk without hobbling and gritting my teeth. I could bend over, use my hands, and stand for hours. I could play with my kids, dance with my husband, work in my gardens, and even wash my floors. This was fantastic! Life was good again.

The Curse

Many months later, Dr. Stacey gave me some troubling news: "I am so sorry, Roxanne, but the medication has been taken off the market. I know that it is the only medication that has worked for you, but I am no longer able to prescribe it."

"But you don't understand," I pleaded. "I can walk and pick up my kids again; I am not in excruciating pain; I can actually function. I have to have it." She handed me a grocery bag full of pharmaceutical samples.

"I know that none of these work for you, but it's all I've got. By the time you are thirty-five, you will be in a wheelchair for the rest of your life," she said. "I wish you all the best. It's been nice meeting you," she smiled as she opened the office door.

What? Wheelchair? Oh, no. No, NO, NO! I screamed in my head.

Hell No!

There is no way I will ever get in a wheelchair. Not now, not ever! *God*, I cried, *there must be something on this green earth that You have created to help me. I cannot go back to the way I was. There must be something that can help me.* The medical community had given up on me. There was no treatment, no hope. All I had was a bag of pharmaceutical samples and a diagnosis of an autoimmune disease that was ravishing my body, destroying my relationships, and ruining my life. As I stood there gobsmacked, with my four-year-old son holding my hand, I looked at him and something welled up inside of me. There was no way I would not be there for him; I was only thirty-two years old. There was no way I was getting in any wheelchair! How dare she say that to me? "I don't think so," I said to her. "There is no way in hell I am ever getting in a wheelchair. I have four little kids who need me. There has to be another way."

> *"There is no way in hell I am ever getting in a wheelchair."*

Dr. Stacey smiled at me as she gave my arm a little squeeze and walked away. "Take good care of yourself," she said as she discharged me from her care. There was no "see you next month," no follow-up appointment, no instructions other than a bag of pharmaceutical samples. After nearly four years I had been abandoned by my rheumatologist. I was alone. With no medical solution in sight, it was just God and me. I was afraid of the pain. But even more so, I was terrified that I would not be able to walk, play with my kids, garden, or live a functional life. What would that mean for me and my family? How could I stop this? What could I do? I was determined that I would find a way and that this would not be my lot in life. I would not be ruled by this disease.

Sometimes we don't know the answer, and sometimes the doctor doesn't know the answer either. Occasionally, we even refuse to see the answer that is right before our eyes. When we are in pain, our vision becomes clouded because all we can focus on is the pain that we are in, either physically or emotionally. This ongoing pain creates stress. When we are chronically stressed, panicked, or riddled with fear, we can no longer think rationally. Therefore, the questions we ask ourselves while in this panic mode are less than inquisitive. They are usually self-reflective and self-focused, such as *Why is this happening to me?* or, *What did I do wrong to deserve this?* These questions don't really help us find the answers we are looking for. The answers that our brain gives us do not help because the questions are not solution-based. They aren't conducive to finding an answer to resolve the pain. This line of questioning focuses on something that is totally subjective and opinionated, which gives you the exact answer you are looking for. Your brain responds with painful emotional answers, such as you are worthless, unloved, stupid, guilty, unworthy, unvalued, rejected, and every other self-sabotaging, demeaning, demoralizing emotion that we can use to add more fuel to our pain and give heightened meaning to our problem. Giving irrational meaning to our problem does not provide an answer; it is just an illogical diagnosis. Therefore, we rarely see the way out of our pain and suffering. Telling yourself that you are worthless and rejected does not bring you any closer to finding a solution for your pain. It intensifies the emotion, causing more pain as you focus even more on the problem.

To find the way out, we must remove the emotion from the pain so we can think logically and look for solutions, not out of fear, but out of the possibility that the solution will provide pleasure. When looking for pleasure, we instinctively become more inquisitive and creative, and our stress decreases. Then our suffering decreases as we are no longer "frozen stiff" in fear. Asking "How can I" or "What else is possible" questions brings a completely different thought process. It is interactive and engaging and causes us to look for answers that drive us forward, toward experiencing pleasure and life once more.

What if I choose to believe that life is happening for me, not to me?

I spent too much of my life frozen by pain, worry, and stress from asking, "What did I do to deserve this" or "Why is this happening" questions. The reality is, bad things happen to good people, and good things happen to bad people. What if I reevaluated what was happening? What if I choose to believe that life is happening for me, not to me?

What if there was a beautiful learning opportunity in every situation or circumstance, just waiting to be discovered to set us free? What if all the horrible things that have ever happened could be reimagined by using different language and by changing the meaning of what happened to give us more power and strength rather than using defeatist language that crushes our soul and leads us down the highway toward pain and destruction?

There is always a solution. There is always a way to improve the situation we are in, and it starts with what we are focusing on and our interpretation of what is happening. Really painful things happen to all of us. But the situation, circumstance, or person involved does not need to burn our life raft. In fact, they don't even have the power to do that. The only power they have is the power we give them by focusing on them. Focusing incessantly on the pain that we are experiencing, whether physically, emotionally, or relationally, causes the pain to consume and overwhelm us, ultimately destroying our peace, hope, joy, and love. It is interesting how we do not know what we have until we lose it—how we take walking, sitting, dancing, bending, and lifting for granted, and in a "suddenly" moment, it can all be stolen from us. But amazingly, in a moment it can all be restored. Sometimes we are just on the other side of a breakthrough when we give up, rather than push through to our victory.

I've learned two important things in my sixteen years of clinical practice and over twenty years of my own healing journey. First, people don't pay attention to their health and wellness until it is nearly too late. Second, audacity, consistency, and grit make the difference between those who conquer the diagnosis and those who are conquered by sickness and disease.

Perhaps God intervened and withdrew that medication to save my life. Is it possible that I was meant to discover how to heal myself so that I could inspire others to do the same? Is it possible that I already had access to everything I needed to heal myself but couldn't see the possibilities?

Lightbulb Moments to Build Audacity

1. Never roll over and agree with or accept any prognosis/diagnosis less than abundant life.

2. You can do anything you want, including finding a way to thrive in any situation, if you want it bad enough.

3. We must ask better questions, refuse to take no for an answer, and be willing to question doctors, specialists, and professionals to audaciously go after finding our own solutions. The solution must be right for you, not someone else's opinion. No one else gets to live your life for you.

Audacious Actions to Live Well on Purpose

1. Decide right now that your life is worth living to the fullest every day. Journal why it is important for you to live life out loud. How will living this way impact you, your family, and the world around you?

2. Decide that you are not the diagnosis. Journal five positive things that define you and why they are important to you.

3. Choose to get up, shower, and get dressed every day, no matter what, starting right now.

CHAPTER 5

But God

MAY 20, 2007, was my thirty-fifth birthday. I woke up excited because my team was leading worship at church. For the past two years, I had loved being a part of the worship team as a vocalist and prayer leader. I cherished the opportunity to be a catalyst to help people experience God on a deeper level. When I tried to get out of bed that morning, I realized that I could not move. Every fiber of my being was screaming at me not to move. The pain was astronomical. It was overwhelming. I was locked, frozen, engulfed by pain in every joint of my body. No matter how frantically I tried, I simply could not get out of bed. My body would not allow it. The clock was ticking, and there I lay, crying, shaking, and sweating from my attempts to get up. Eventually my Mr. Wonderful came into the room to see what I was doing since it was nearly time to leave. He stood at the bedside looking helplessly at me, not able to offer any assistance.

I told him to take the kids to church without me, insisting that I was fine. With the house quiet, I lay there all alone in my bed, praying to God to take the pain away and help me get up. Suddenly I realized that the curse my rheumatologist had spoken over me three years earlier was trying to come true. How could this be? No! There was no way in hell I was going to allow this to be my lot in life. I was never getting in that wheelchair! I had to figure out how to get out of this bed.

I began to cry out loud to God to help me: "Lord Jesus, heal me. Take this pain away." I commanded my body to get up. "Thank You for healing me, Jesus," I declared over and over. Yet minute after minute, hour after hour, there was no change. When my family arrived home from church, the pain was just as it had been when I woke up, and I was desperate for a washroom. I was convinced that if something did not happen soon, there was going to be a major accident all over my bed. I could not allow this to happen. I couldn't embarrass myself like that. Scott stood there staring at me while I cried in anguish as I repeatedly tried to get up. Because of the pain and how locked down my back and hips were, no one could touch me. He tried to help pull me up, but my back would go into full spasm and it felt as though my spine would snap in half. I had to do this alone. Even if it broke me, I would get up.

With every fiber of my being, I summoned the strength of Samson and with sheer grit, screaming in agony, sat up on the edge of the bed. I tried to stand, but my hips and pelvis started spasming, as they couldn't bear the weight. I could not fail. I could not have an accident in my marital bed. I had to make this happen. I finally heaved myself up, tears pouring down my face, gritting my teeth and grabbing the bed as my crutch. I threw my body forward toward the bathroom. I desperately tried to convince my mind and my body that this was possible. It was only ten steps.

Every step was a monumental feat engulfed in anguish. Every step seemed like it took hours. As I made my way down the side of the bed, eventually there was no more bed to grab onto. Out of the corner of my eye, I spied a roll of wrapping paper leaning up against the wall. I reached for it and used it as a cane. At long last, I arrived at the toilet. I turned around, ready to collapse onto the seat, when I realized that the problem had shifted. Now I could not sit down. My hips were totally locked. I could not sit down, but I couldn't stay standing, because my body was on the verge of collapsing. I felt panicked. "Come on, come on!" I cried. "Relax, relax, you can do this. Unlock, unlock," I told myself, bobbing up and down to try to unlock my hips. Finally something shifted, and in utter relief I sat down. I had made it. I did not embarrass myself or leave a mess for my husband to clean up. We were both relieved.

After I was finished going to the washroom, I realized that I couldn't get off the toilet. My hips were now locked in the seated position, and they would not unlock as I was desperately trying to stand. What was happening to me? Why was my body not working properly? The pain had been one thing, but this? This was a whole different ball game.

This episode began years of the unruly, unmanageable game I called "negotiating with my body." I spent the next many years trying to convince my body to move the way I wanted it to. To sit when I wanted it to sit. To stand when I asked it to. To walk when I commanded it to. And most importantly, to try and look "normal" in the process, without drawing negative attention to myself.

The negative attention came in all sorts of ways—the glares, the double takes, the looks of disgust, rude comments, and name-calling, usually from total strangers for no reason at all. I would be standing in the checkout lane at the grocery store minding my own business when someone standing behind me in line would say in their out-loud voice, "Why are you standing like that? What is wrong with you?" as they looked at me in disgust. It would have been compassionate if they were concerned about me; however, the tone of their voice and the look on their face as they rolled their eyes at me told a very different story.

Healing by Faith

An amazing man of God came to our church on June 3, 2007. Two weeks after the horrific experience of not being able to get out of my bed, it was my team's turn to lead worship at church again. I wanted to be a part of this Sunday's service because our guest speaker was going to be talking about the healing power of Jesus. Since I needed healing, I needed to be there. The pain was still unbearable that morning, but I was getting better at making my body conform to moving, and I did not take no for an answer. With my teeth gritted and a smile pasted to my face to try and cover up the anguish, we made our way to church.

Just standing to do the twenty-minute worship set took me to my maximum level of pain tolerance, with sweat running down my back from the exertion to stay upright. I worshiped as though my life depended on it. When it was time for the sermon, I got down from the platform and took my seat next to my Mr. Wonderful to listen to our guest speaker, all the while hoping that I would be able to stand and get back up to the platform to finish the service without drawing too much attention to myself and creating a scene as I negotiated with my body to move.

The speaker, Dennis, was a powerful speaker, and the presence of God was on him. The truth that he spoke and the testimonies he gave of seeing healing miracles of God were awe-inspiring. Dennis described Jesus in a way I had never heard before. The depth, the expanse, the lengths to which Jesus reaches out in mercy and compassion to heal moved me to my core. I fell in love with Jesus all over again. I believed it was possible to be healed. I knew it was possible, of that I had been fully convinced. There was no doubt in my mind.

When Dennis finished speaking, he invited those who needed healing to come up after the service and he would lay hands on people and pray for their healing. When I heard this, my spirit leapt within me. I was so excited! This holy man would pray for me if I came forward? This man who knew Jesus so intimately would pray for me to be healed? I was giddy with excitement. I could feel both fireworks and butterflies inside my belly at the same time. *This is my chance,* I thought. *I could get fully healed today!* But something strange happened. As quickly as I felt the excitement, I heard a voice inside my head say, *How dare you ask this man to pray for you? Look around you, look at all the people here who are sicker than you, who need this man's help. How dare you take up his time.* I looked around at all the people in the congregation. About five hundred people were there that day. I felt defeated. I was grieved at the thought of losing my chance to have this anointed man of God pray for me and be healed.

I stood up, negotiated with my body to unlock my pelvis and hips, and willed my legs to walk. Gripping my thighs to hold myself upright, I made my way back to the altar, finished the closing worship set, and made my way back down to our pew to collect my things to leave. My soul was crying inside. I was devastated that I would not be getting prayed for today and would miss out on my opportunity to receive a divine miracle. It was as if I had a magnificent gift before me that I was not allowed to unwrap because of a whisper I heard in my mind that sounded like truth. It was a lie from the pit of hell that I heard in my mind and accepted as truth, a decoy sent to distract me from getting healing.

Then the most amazing thing happened. A group of my friends and colleagues gathered around me and insisted that I go up for prayer. I told them that I could not waste Dennis's time, that others were in way more need than me and he was busy helping them.

"That is ridiculous," they said as they grabbed my arms and pulled me to the front of the church where Dennis was standing talking with some people. Interrupting him, they

It was a lie from the pit of hell that I heard in my mind and accepted as truth, a decoy sent to distract me from getting healing.

pushed me right in front of him and said, "Dennis, this is Roxanne, our office administrator, she is in so much pain, she really needs your prayers." I was the sickest person there that day, and I knew that. I needed the prayer, but the lying enemy had tried to deceive me and trick me into not receiving my healing. Now here I was standing before this man of God who believed in the power of healing and miracles more than anyone I had ever met. His presence was calming, loving, accepting. There was no judgment, no condescending looks, no meanness in him. I felt safe and had absolute trust and faith that God was there with him. With all the love and compassion of heaven itself, Dennis looked at me, smiled, and placed his hands gently on the top of my head. Then with striking authority he commanded, "In the name of Jesus, I command all pain to go now." And it did! Not just a little tiny bit, but all of it. All the pain left my body instantly. It simply disappeared. I was shocked.

"How do you feel, Roxanne?" Dennis asked.

"I do not have any pain. It's all gone!" I exclaimed.

"Praise God!" Dennis shouted. As we chatted, one of the associate pastors joined in our lively discussion. He started explaining the challenges with my spine and limited range of motion to Dennis, trying to emphasize how bad things were for me. Dennis did not seem concerned at all. He talked about how God is faithful to finish the work that He starts, and that Jesus is the Healer. "You know, Roxanne," Dennis said as he was packing up his things, "God has more for you. I believe that this is just the start of your healing. There is a healing prayer clinic in Ottawa that is open every Friday. I want you to go this Friday afternoon between 1 and 4 p.m. I will let them know that you are coming to get the rest of your healing."

"Okay," I said, unsure, excited, and a little scared because I had no understanding for what a prayer clinic would be like. *This was my time*, I assured myself. I was going to get fully healed! I had no pain, but I was still walking strangely, and my mobility had not improved. I was going to go to the healing clinic, and no one was going to stop me. I was on top of the world as we went home. I had been in so much pain that morning, and now it was gone. I felt fantastic, so I went outside and hand-dug my massive vegetable garden and planted it all, pain-free. Scott was shocked; he could not believe what he was seeing. How was it possible for me to be digging and planting any garden, let alone that massive one? In the evening after I had finished planting, I asked him what he thought about my newfound freedom from pain. "Did you see me dig up and plant my garden?"

"Yup," he said.

"Isn't it awesome?" I asked.

"I don't understand," he said. "I don't get it. You could hardly move this morning."

"And now I can, without pain," I said with enthusiasm. Looking at his countenance, I could tell he was not as excited as I was. "What's wrong? Why aren't you happy for me?" I asked.

"I am happy for you; I just don't get it," he replied.

I didn't understand why or how he could have this reaction; all I knew was that I didn't have any pain, and that was a miracle! A few days later Scott went out of town on business. I was working as my church's office administrator while I was completing my natural health studies, and that Friday the office was all astir. My colleagues were all asking me if I was really going to go to the Healing Clinic. To each one I would say, "Yes, I have to go. I am nervous, but I have to go and see if I get totally healed. This might be my only chance."

One of my friends who had been part of my miracle on Sunday said, "Roxanne, you might fall down, and none of us will be there with you. What if you get hurt? How will you get home? I heard things like that happen at these kinds of places."

"What do you mean, fall down?" I asked, pie-eyed.

"You know, being 'slain in the spirit.' People can fall down when they feel God's presence," she stated matter-of-factly. I didn't really know what that meant, but I was going to get my healing even if I fell down.

"I'll be okay," I told them. But the truth was, falling down made me nervous. So nervous that I took my time going to the healing clinic. By the time I got home from work, I had convinced myself not to go at all. Then I felt guilty because Dennis told them I was coming. *I'll drive super slowly. Maybe they will be closed by the time I get there,* I thought to myself.

Desperation sets in when physical pain, emotional turmoil, and mental anguish become inescapable. When we are in constant pain, we can lose our center, our faith, and our hope. This affects our ability to find peace and joy from within. Some good people walk away from living altogether and enter the realm of the walking dead, void of life, happiness, love, compassion, and hope. Others press into life, searching for answers, solutions, wisdom, and faith. Faith kept me alive. Faith keeps me alive. I talk to God endlessly throughout the day and night—communing with Him, beholding Him, delighting in His mercy and grace. Faith is the evidence of things not yet seen, making faith elusive and uncertain for many as they want the proof. Seeing the proof is fact, not faith. We don't get faith from facts. We develop and foster faith through believing it is possible despite the evidence at hand.

> *We develop and foster faith through believing it is possible despite the evidence at hand.*

Dennis had spoken into the depths of my soul that Sunday. He released my soul from the prison of torment and allowed my spirit to connect with heaven, the realm of all possibility—the realm where, if you see it, you can have it, all for the small fee of faith. I was going to the Healing Clinic with a fresh dose of faith, expecting my miracle. This was going to be amazing!

Lightbulb Moments to Build Audacity

1. Mindset is everything. Making a decision in your mind and locking it down is powerful and can move pain, impossibility, and mountains.

2. Sometimes we more readily listen to and accept lies than the truth.

3. The Enemy's voice can sound a lot like your own. Be sure to validate your thoughts against the truth.

Audacious Actions to Live Well on Purpose

1. Follow your gut, even if it is scary. What are two things that you know deep inside that you should do to uplevel your wellness but have not yet acted on? Write them down and decide to commit to doing them no matter what. Then take the first step.

2. Keep moving. It is hard to move when your body or the pain says no. Move despite the pain, even if it's seated leg raises, chair jumping jacks, or wall push-ups. When you stop moving, you lose the ability to move as the muscles and ligaments atrophy and contract. Keep the mobility that you have and try to increase it through simple daily exercises that you can do at home.

3. Refuse to let other people's fear squash your faith. Fear can hold you back from your greatest breakthrough. You need to believe it is possible. It is not up to your family or friends to believe for you, and you do not need anyone else's approval to have your own faith. They are not living in your body. Journal about the areas of your health that you need to stand in a greater level of faith. Sign your name as a commitment to start walking in faith today.

CHAPTER 6

Healing by Faith

I ARRIVED at the healing clinic at 3:55 p.m. The clinic closed at 4:00 p.m. I sat in my car with crazy emotions racing through my body. I was excited and it felt like my heart was leaping for joy. I was nervous and felt as if I was having a small panic attack. I was laughing. Why? I had no idea. I was crying, and I was afraid. *What was going to happen? Should I go in?* I felt like I was totally losing it. *What was going on? Why was I having all these emotions and how could they all be happening at the same time?* I could feel doubt creeping in and was beginning to think that this was a ridiculous idea. I just wanted to go home. Wait, no, I didn't! I desperately wanted to go inside and see what would happen. *Would God be in this place? Would this healing clinic be everything that Dennis had told me about?* I wanted to go inside and get my miracle, but I was a total basket case. I could not get

"Lord Jesus, I am coming to meet You today."

a grip on my emotions—or my heart rate. My heart was leaping out of my chest. I was on the verge of driving away when something snapped inside me. *You have to do this*, I thought to myself. I threw open the car door and said out loud, "Lord Jesus, I am coming to meet You today." I took a deep breath, opened the door, went into the healing clinic, and instantly felt peace in my body and mind.

The receptionist greeted me and asked me to fill out a form. She told me that Dennis had told them that I was coming, and that they had been waiting for me. She led me down an exceptionally long hallway to a small room. Inside were three beautiful older women who were smiling at me and welcoming me to come in and sit down. They put their hands on me and started praying. I could feel a warm blanket of love and peace fall all over me. I felt like I was wrapped up in the arms of God. I had never experienced anything like this before. It was breathtaking. I was sobbing, and tears were flowing down my cheeks. I felt safe, protected, loved, seen, and heard. A million pounds of emotional shame, torment, guilt, ugliness, and pain were lifted off my shoulders and back. I felt euphoric.

About thirty minutes later, the prayer time concluded. I can't even tell you what the ladies said or what they prayed. It was as if they did not actually exist. The women asked me how I felt. Without assessing anything in my body, I just knew that I had met Jesus that afternoon, that He had touched me and made me whole. "I am healed," I said as a matter of fact. "Thank you! Thank you! Thank you so much! Praise God!" I said.

The women gave me a prescription on a recipe card to read three scriptures every night before bed. I got up and left the room, floating on heaven's love. I hobbled down that long hallway the same way I went in, yet I was totally unfazed by how I was walking. Seemingly nothing had changed—until I got into the parking lot. I took a step off the curb and thought, *Wow, that felt different.* I took another step and got excited as I felt a freedom in my steps that I had not felt for quite some time. Something *was* different. I was walking differently; I was not limping. *Well, that's cool*, I thought as I got into my minivan.

Still elated and feeling fantastic, I started the long drive home. As I turned onto the freeway, I was shocked to suddenly feel my lungs inflate with oxygen. *"Oh, my! I can breathe!"* I inhaled again, and I could feel my lungs inflate deeply, something I had not felt for way too long. How long? Long enough that I noticed that I was actually breathing. Ankylosing spondylitis (AS) is a disease that fuses the spine together and causes what is known as a bamboo spine, a rigidity that causes limited range of motion and movement. If you have ever seen an elderly person walking so bent over that they are looking at the ground rather than straight ahead, you have witnessed the devastating effects of AS. In the process of fusing your spine it also crushes your internal organs, leading to serious breathing and cardiovascular problems. Looking back, it's comical that I was so happy when I thought I was not dying when that radiologist confirmed the diagnosis of AS because it's an insidious, painful, debilitating death over a long period. It's a gradual loss of function that many don't see or pay attention to until it's already gone.

When did I stop breathing normally? I don't know. It was just something that seemed to slip away as the days and months went on. Slowly over time I noticed that I could not take deep breaths. Have you ever laughed so hard that you laugh without making a sound right before you draw in a huge breath of air? I love laughing that hard. I love it when something is just so funny that it takes my breath away. Over time, I couldn't take in that deep breath and would end up coughing and choking instead, which always made the joke less funny as people started to panic and ask me if I was okay. When I noticed I was breathing better, I wasn't trying to see if I was breathing better. I just felt it. When I realized I could actually breathe deeply, I laughed out loud at this awesome bonus miracle. "Lord Jesus, thank You for infusing me with the breath of life straight from the throne room of heaven. Thank You for filling my lungs with life, even though I didn't ask for it."

I got home past dinnertime. With my Mr. Wonderful being out of town, I was flying solo with the kids. So once I was home and in mommy mode, I didn't really think about what had happened at the healing clinic or the discoveries I had made on my way home. Life with four kids was busy; there was always something or someone who needed attention. Late that night as I was crawling into bed, I remembered the scripture prescription the ladies had given me. The prayer team had told me to read each one out loud before going to bed every night so that I could hear the scriptures, not just read them. They had read to me Romans 10:17, which says, "Now faith comes by hearing, and hearing by the word of God." Simply put, hearing the scriptures out loud is what increases our faith. I took out the recipe card and looked up the scriptures in my Bible: Matthew 8:16–17, Mark 16:16–18, and 1 Peter 2:24. I read each scripture out loud with passion, closed my Bible, and went to sleep.

I had a wonderful sleep. I woke up feeling very refreshed and alive. The house was quiet so the kids were either still sleeping or, more likely, watching Saturday morning cartoons. I got up and went to get ready for my day. I was standing in the bathroom brushing my teeth, thinking about all the things that needed to be done that day, when I saw something strange in the mirror. I seemed taller and it wasn't because I was wearing shoes. Since Dennis had prayed for me, I no longer needed to wear those ugly sandals all the time. The sink seemed to have shrunk. *What in the world?* I thought as I turned to my side to get a better look.

For the past three years, I had been standing sideways in the full-length mirror, commanding my shoulders to go back and to stand up straight. No matter how hard I tried to push my shoulders back and stand erect, nothing ever changed. I seemed to be locked in a forward position with my shoulders hunched over. But today? Today as I looked in the mirror, I was standing up straight! I could not believe my eyes. I looked and looked, I changed positions, I changed sides. Was I really seeing what I was seeing? Was I dreaming? My Mr. Wonderful was not home so I couldn't ask him.

Excited, nervous, and baffled, I ran into the living room. The only child who was awake was my ten-year-old daughter. She was on the living room floor playing with her Barbies. "Do you notice anything different about Mommy today?" I asked as I spun around in circles in front of her. In less than five seconds, my sweet little girl excitedly confirmed what I had been thinking.

"Mommy! Your back! Your back is straight!"

"Yes, it is!" I exclaimed with great joy. "Jesus healed me!" She went running to tell the other kids, and I cried tears of immense joy. I had gone to the healing clinic even though my friends and coworkers tried to convince me not to, and I got my miracle. I told Jesus that I was coming to meet with Him, and He met me.

I told Jesus that I was coming to meet with Him, and He met me.

I was flying on cloud nine for the entire weekend. I felt a newfound sense of freedom in my body and in my movements. I was able to easily get down on my hands and knees to scrub the floors, something that had been nearly impossible just a week before. When my Mr. Wonderful called to check in on me and the kids, I did not say anything about my healing. I wanted to surprise him. I wanted to see if he would notice anything different about the way that I stood or walked when he saw me. The anticipation was exciting! I could not wait for him to come home and see me standing straight and tall!

That Sunday at church, most of my friends were excited for me. They wanted to know everything that had happened and what it felt like. They were amazed at my stature and the way I was able to move. I told everyone I spoke to on Sunday that they should go to the Healing Clinic too. I was now an absolute believer in the power of miracles and healing, and that it was for everyone. I always had thought of God as a superhero. I always felt that He could and would do anything that we asked for. God is good, and now I had tangible proof.

Some of my friends were skeptical about my healing. They wanted to "wait and see" if I was really healed. One friend took me aside and challenged me, saying that I was making it up, that there had to be a scientific explanation why I was suddenly standing taller and not in pain anymore. I explained to him that there was no scientific explanation. My spine was partially fused, and I had X-rays proving it. Now it felt like it was no longer fused because I was more flexible, my back was straight, and I was not in pain. I explained that ankylosing spondylitis is an autoimmune disease that doesn't go away on its own. He was livid. He called me a liar and stormed off. I was surprised to see that some people cannot handle the truth. I was sad that some people could miss a miracle of God even when it was right before their very own eyes—not just miss it but refuse to believe their own eyes.

Very late Sunday night my Mr. Wonderful came home from his business trip. The kids and I were already in bed. I knew that he would be tired from traveling all day and would have to get up early to get to work, but still, I wanted to show him my transformation. I could feel my heart pounding out of my chest. I had butterflies in my stomach. Would he notice? Would he scream with delight? Would he cry with joy? I waited until he got into bed and I told him that I had something to show him. I got up and stood in the light in the hallway where he would be able to see me clearly.

Silence.

I turned around in a circle, one way and then the other. I smiled and gave my best "ta-da!" hand signal. Nothing. Scott was silent. I could tell that he was looking at me. His eyes were open. Was he not seeing it? Could he not see any difference in the way I stood and moved?

"Babe, do you see it? Do you see that I am standing up straight?" I inquired.

"Yup," he said, with all the emotion of a rock.

Confused, I asked, "Aren't you happy for me?"

"Yes, but I don't understand," he said.

"What do you mean you don't understand? Jesus healed me. I went to the healing clinic on Friday, and I woke up like this on Saturday morning."

"I can see that. I just don't understand how it happened.

I left and you were one way, and I came home and you are another. I don't get it," he stated.

"You don't believe that I am healed?" I pouted.

"No, it's not that. I am just really tired and really confused, and I just want to go to sleep. I've had a very long day. I have to get up early," he said as he pulled the covers up.

My heart was shattered. Why was he not happy for me? Maybe I should have told him over the phone to prepare him for my healing. After all, it was a major change, and he doesn't really like surprises, but this one was just so good that I wanted to tell him in person. I wanted him to see for himself. I went to bed disappointed. How could he not be excited? This was the miracle we had been waiting for. I was heartbroken.

The next night my husband and I had an argument about my healing. Not so much about me being healed but about his total confusion and inability to explain what happened. My Mr. Wonderful is a Christian. He had been going to church his whole life. But he had never witnessed a faith healing, and it was not something that was talked about in the church he attended growing up. As a very logical and rational person, he had no comprehension for what had happened. There was no logical rationalization for what had happened to me. He had left home and I was one way, and he came home and I was made new.

"The ways of God are foolish to man," I recited from a scripture that I knew, "but that doesn't make them less real.

You cannot access God in your mind. God is Spirit, and we must meet Him there, in the spiritual realm, not in the realm of the thinking mind. I just don't understand why you are not happy for me," I said, exacerbated.

"I am happy for you; I just don't get it," my Mr. Wonderful reiterated. "I just don't know what to think."

"Well, how about thinking that you are happy for me," I said as I began to cry.

Confused, I went outside to water my gardens. I just didn't understand. Here I am, healed, and my husband was more worried about his theology making sense than me being healed.

We didn't speak about the healing I had received for many years. The healing theology was something that we didn't agree on, but he could not deny the physical, emotional, and spiritual changes in me. My Mr. Wonderful supported me on my faith journey, encouraging me to go to the Healing Clinic weekly, saying that he knew I always felt better after I went for prayer. He was right. There was something wonderfully magnificent about being prayed over and feeling the presence of the Holy Spirit as waves of warmth and love fell over me. I eagerly anticipated the scripture prescriptions that brought me closer to Jesus. The angry, bitter, depressed me was dead. I had been raised to new life and a new love. I was filled with peace and hope. I was happy. Theology did not matter. People's opinions did not matter. I was free, and nothing could change that. Our marriage blossomed in every way, including our intimacy.

Lightbulb Moments to Build Audacity

1. Follow your heart. Your heart always knows the next step in the journey. Listen wisely.

2. We create our own happiness. Happiness is not contingent on someone else being happy for us or not, accepting us or not, agreeing with us or not. Happiness comes from peace and joy within.

3. You do not require a scientific explanation. Scientific explanations do nothing more than explain what is seen and understood by the human mind. Faith sees when there is nothing evidential to assess.

Audacious Actions to Live Well on Purpose

1. Look up one of the scriptures that was given to me: Matthew 8:16–17; Mark 16:16–18; or 1 Peter 2:24. Read it out loud three times a day for a week. Journal how it makes you feel.

2. Choose happiness despite the circumstances or people around you. You get to choose your mood, so choose a mood that is life-giving, not life-sucking. When you catch yourself in a funk, think about or, better yet, get up and do something that brings a smile to your face.

3. The next time you have butterflies in your stomach or feel nervous about a situation, assess whether it is nervous excitement or an actual protective response. Many times, we misplace nervous excitement for fear and end up not following through with an opportunity that can change our life for the better. Dig deep inside and ask yourself if this is really something to be afraid of or concerned about. If not, take a deep breath and go for it.

CHAPTER 7

Sticks, Stones, and Bullies: The Impact of Names

"STICKS AND STONES may break my bones, but names will never hurt me." I sang this rhyme many times in my younger years to try and shrug off the crude, belittling, and hurtful remarks of other kids. The truth is that *names* always hurt. I spent hours and days thinking, rethinking, analyzing, and going through what had happened—what they said, what I said, trying to make a better scenario in my mind where I won and my dignity was preserved, but mostly trying to not let the name-calling bother me and ruin my day. Name-calling sent me spinning. Sometimes it was a blip in my day, sometimes it was a crater that I spent the next week crawling out of. To overcome name-calling, we must be able to stand in the truth of who we are. Only then will we know that what others are saying is not true, and the names won't cut us, leaving scars.

As a healthcare practitioner, I see firsthand how deeply words wound people. People know that name-calling hurts; that is why they do it. Name-calling is a mind game. At face value, there is really nothing tangible about a harsh word other than perhaps the crudeness or stigma attached to it. Name-calling strikes at our pride, self-esteem, and sense of worth.

When we feel worthless or devalued, it shakes us at our core because we all have a fear of being rejected and a deep fear of not being loved. Name-calling tests our sense of acceptance and worth, not just from a peer point of view but from an internal perspective. If we do not accept ourselves—if we do not feel that we are worthy, worthwhile, or loved—then we cannot expect it from others. I have counseled countless women to whom words were spoken ten, twenty, even forty years ago that elicited an emotional response as strong as if those words had been said that very moment. I have seen how a woman's value, ego, personality, and very existence was formed and shaped by the names she was called as a child, teen, and young adult. I have seen how names have robbed women of all ages of a beautiful and purpose-filled life.

Every woman is redeemable. But until the woman believes that she has value and worth, until she believes that she is lovable and accepted, it is incredibly challenging to make headway because her default mindset may be filled with lies, false beliefs and fear—fear of not fitting in, fear of being an outcast, fear of never finding true love—forgetting all the while that acceptance, love, and worth come from within. It is impossible to genuinely love, value, and accept another person if we do not love, value, and accept ourselves.

I came up with a new rhyme to sing that makes more sense:

Sticks and stones may break my bones, but names hurt me even more.

Sticks and stones damage the physical body. Names and words have an impact on our soul, which is our mind, our will, and our emotions. Some women can be brutally beaten and get back up, pretending to shake it off and move on. Many women can be called a name and be scarred at the deepest level, affecting every part of their existence, until they are able to release the imprint of that name off their soul. But that seems easier said than done. Sadly, many women do not have just one name-calling experience; they have numerous. Sometimes they are called names so often that they start believing these things about themselves, when nothing could be further from the truth. Getting women to believe better about themselves and who they really are deep down inside is crucial to healing and freedom. But this is where the resistance is. Women who have been perpetually called names or slandered have a difficult time shifting their mindsets because they now believe those degrading names, words, or qualities are true.

What's in a name? A name on its own holds nothing. It is meaningless until we give it definition, meaning, and animation. It is our choice to agree with and accept the attack on our soul. Many choose to agree with words that someone speaks over them rather than believe what they know about who they are deep down inside. If you would never ask them for their opinion on an important life event, then why would you concern yourself with their critical, condescending, and untruthful comments? Think and believe more highly of yourself. This is not being proud. This does not lack humility. You know who you are and what you stand for, believe in, and value. You know your heart, your dreams, your passions, and your own brilliance. You may not be everyone's cup of tea, and that is okay. We can't be BFFs with everyone. Just because someone does not like you doesn't mean something is wrong with you or that you are a lesser person.

In most instances, disdain of another person usually comes from a place of jealousy, guilt, or shame from the insulting individual. The reality is that they see something in you they desire and think is out of their reach, or they see a characteristic they possess that they do not like about themselves, which causes them to resort to taunting, bullying, shaming, slandering, and name-calling to try and bring you down below their assumed level in society, like an imaginary pecking order. Contemptuous people try to pull you down to lift themselves up. When you know who you are, no one can cause you to fall and lose all sense of yourself, your value, and who you were created to be, and the name-calling will be irrelevant.

I am not suggesting that it is easy because it is not. Far too many women carry around way too much baggage from their past from vain name-callers, bullies, and condescending, disrespectful people. How many times has someone said something that immediately caused you to think about a situation from years ago where something similar happened and that memory caused you to immediately back off, back up, and shut up rather than stand tall in your rightful power, purpose, and radiance? Rather than stand in the truth of who you know you are and your innate awesomeness, you agree with the deceitful lie, and another leaf shrivels on the branches of your soul. When more and more leaves shrivel on your branches, your radiance and beauty become suppressed, which causes you to go into a winter season of the soul, where you become a dark shadow of your former self and your heart begins to grow cold—first toward yourself and then toward those around you.

Winter Seasons Can Be Very Lonely

Winter seasons are difficult to explain to those around us, including our loved ones, simply because they do not see us the way we have chosen to revisualize ourselves based on the disdainful eyes of a bully, or worse, ourselves. Your spouse cannot see what you are choosing to see, because they have never seen you that way; it is a foreign concept to them. The personality you are choosing to become is not the person they know and love. Their lack of understanding, compassion, or empathy for the situation is not because they don't love you, and it is not because they don't acknowledge that what was said was demeaning and horrible. They don't understand why you are so upset because they love you and see you for who you are, deep down inside, and they don't understand why you don't see yourself the same way. They do not understand why you would agree with what was said. They cannot help you climb out of that pit because they cannot see what you are talking about. It is not their experience of you, and they have no frame of reference for the fabricated identity that you are trying to wear as your own.

We bully ourselves all the time. When we say things such as, *Look at me. I am hideous; no wonder people make fun of me!* your loved ones do look at you. They do see you. But what they do not see is a person that resembles anything even remotely hideous. You are beautiful to your spouse, inside and out. The only person who can get you out of the winter season is you. When we think differently and see differently, then we can act differently. The way you see yourself, your unique perspective, is what either keeps you in the winter season or ushers in your spring.

The way you see yourself, your unique perspective, is what either keeps you in the winter season or ushers in your spring.

I had many instances of being bullied as an adult due to the deformities in my body from the disease. My Mr.

Wonderful could never understand why these episodes upset me so much. He thought that I was exaggerating how I was being treated until one day when my husband, our four kids, three foster kids, and I had just finished serving at our church's Maundy Thursday service, which is the commemoration of the Last Supper Jesus had with His disciples before He was betrayed and crucified. During this service, our church offers a handwashing service. My Mr. Wonderful washed people's hands, and I dried them, blessing each person and gazing into their eyes with love as I held their hands in mine, praying over them for healing, peace, hope, and life.

After church, we went to a local coffee shop for a treat. We pulled up in two separate cars and headed in as one extra-large family. The kids were chattering about what they were going to get and asking questions and pointing at the menu. Distracted by all seven kids asking questions at the same time, I didn't notice two women who had been at that evening's service seated in the corner on the other side of the restaurant until I heard one of them call out to me from across the restaurant.

"Hey, Roxanne," she yelled in my direction, "what is wrong with you anyway? Why do you stand that way? What is wrong with your back? Look at you!" she yelled from across the café. Immediately she and her friend started laughing, and not just a little chuckle, but loud, uproarious, exaggerated cackling. By this time, all my kids had stopped talking, and even my Mr. Wonderful had stopped, turned around, and was looking at her. I tried to shrug it off and ignore her by redirecting everyone to place their orders. I spoke louder to try to drown out their laughter. She continued, "You pray for people to get healed; try getting your own healing," she sneered, as she and her friend erupted with laughter. Everyone in the coffee shop was now staring at me, and all I wanted to do was grab my kids and get out of there. I could not imagine what they were thinking, considering what they had just heard. I ignored her as best I could. I tried to adjust my posture to look more "normal," but the reality was that I was so embarrassed for my kids and totally shocked that someone I knew would bully me right in front of my own children. I had just held her hands in mine and blessed her. My soul was crushed. I was embarrassed that my children and husband had to experience this bullying. We quickly finished our order and left the restaurant. No one said anything about what had happened. I am not sure whether they just did not know what to say, or if they were shocked that I was not crying, or if they just didn't want to make matters worse.

Out in the parking lot, I asked Scott if he heard what she had said.

"Yes, what the heck was that?" he asked.

"You never believe that people do this kind of thing to me," I said. I had come home crying on numerous occasions because of a rude or belittling comment made by a stranger for no apparent reason other than the way I stood or walked when I was out in public doing errands. He had always told me that I was exaggerating or that I misinterpreted what happened. "Usually it's a stranger bullying me, not someone who actually knows me. I can't believe she did that, and in front of the kids too! What is wrong with her? We were literally just at church!"

"I don't know. That was just weird. Just forget about it," he said, trying to shrug it off.

Thank God I had grown a lot and knew who I was and could no longer be stepped on and brought to tears. The old me in this situation would have grabbed everyone and run out the door crying. I would have felt sorry for myself for days or even weeks. I would have ignored her at church and tried to avoid her as much as possible. However, the new me had come to peace with the reality that no one knows what anyone else is going through, because no one else has or will ever walk in someone else's shoes. The hard truth is that no one has exactly the same set of circumstances, history, health factors, education, mindset, values, or beliefs as

We all experience our current life based on past experiences.

you. No one was raised the same as you, and no one has the same traumas, fears, or anxieties as you. We all experience our current life based on past experiences.

Your brain is so magnificent that it has catalogued everything that has ever happened to you based on its perception of those events. When something happens to you, whether an experience, event, or circumstance, in a split second your brain subconsciously looks for a historical event, situation, feeling, or circumstance that is similar in some way. Your brain searches for anything that has ever happened to you that looks like, sounds like, feels like, smells like, or tastes like what you are experiencing, and it makes a conclusion about the current situation based on past reference points. Because your brain is always drawing parallels to your past, it can be challenging to overcome fear, anxiety, negativity, guilt, shame, anger, resentment, and any other myriad emotions or moods. We cannot unlearn an automatic subconscious response, even if it no longer serves us or is detrimental to our well-being, but we can rewrite or reprogram the way we respond by forming new neural pathways and emotions with positive associations, emotions, people, events, and even aromas.

In a similar situation, I was teaching a class when one of the attendees suddenly blurted out, "For the love of God, could you please just sit down!"

"Pardon me?" I said with a puzzled look on my face.

"Well, it's clear that you are in a lot of pain. I can't stand looking at you any longer. Please sit down," she said emphatically. I was shocked that not only had she drawn attention to the way I was standing and moving but that she also demanded I sit down to make *her* feel more comfortable. I explained that I had an autoimmune disease that had fused my spine together and that a few months ago I'd had a hip replacement. I was not in any pain, but I was learning to walk again. I chuckled, saying she should have met me years ago when I could hardly walk or stand, that the way I am now is a major improvement. My comments silenced her quickly, but the atmosphere in the room had changed. Someone had run to find me a chair, others encouraged me to sit as well, two ladies apologized for their friend, and one woman even got up and left. It seemed that this interruption was uncomfortable for many of the people.

It bothered me that this woman had called me out in the middle of a presentation because she felt uncomfortable, yet she never asked me if I was okay. There was just an assumption of pain based on how I looked. Although the intention seemed good, it was misplaced. The concern was all about her comfort, disguised in the cloak of mine. It brought a little rain cloud of tears streaming down my face on my way home. It was so discouraging to realize that people still saw me as differently abled after I had worked so hard to improve my health and mobility.

I wish I had known about reframing and giving my experiences a better meaning at that point in my life. If I had been able to look at that interaction in a way that served me and kept me in peace and joy rather than choosing an interpretation that saw it as humiliating, I would have spared myself much grief.

Identifying the Pity Party Mindset

Catching yourself in the pity party mindset is the first step to kicking the negative thought processes and self-defeating mindset out of your life for good. To form new positive pathways of association, we must think better. Mindset is the key

> *In every circumstance or situation, regardless of what was said, done, or thought, only you have the power to think better.*

to success in any area of your life. First, we must believe that we can; then, we must demonstrate that we will do it, no matter what.

In every circumstance or situation, regardless of what was said, done, or thought, only you have the power to think better. It doesn't really matter what anyone says to you to try and pull you out of your funk or debunk the lies of a bully. You are the only one who can snap yourself out of it. We shift gears only when we change our mindset 180 degrees to a more positive perspective, causing us to think better. When we think better, we start feeling better, and when we feel better, our emotional state improves. Then we can get back at the steering wheel of our life.

Have you ever been so down that you just wanted to be left alone, but after a while you wondered why no one was coming to check on you, even though you had told everyone to leave you alone? We are born to be in community with other people. We need nurturing, love, compassion, laughter, and hope to feel alive and connected. When we choose to stay in the corner, we miss out on the connection of community and we miss out on life. No one notices that you are missing out except you. Everyone else goes on with their lives and does not consider the pain they may have caused you. By staying in your dark, lonely corner, you are holding yourself prisoner to what someone else said or did. In the process, you are not living your own life and are missing out on the lives of those around you. The quicker you can identify when you are retreating into an abandoned, forsaken, rejected mindset, the sooner you will be able to think positive, life-giving thoughts about yourself and your situation, shift your mindset, and get back to living.

Speaking a Better Word

The second step to forming a new, positive mindset is to grab hold of the "stinking thinking" and speak a better word. Take a negative thought and replace it with a positive thought. Then speak the better thought out loud—scream it if you must. This is crucial because sometimes when we try to redirect our thoughts, the negativity and lies start firing rapidly in our mind. We have flashbacks of memories and people that try to remind us why we think we are a loser, a failure, or why we are worthy of such disrespect and negativity. We subconsciously gather all the historical evidence against us and play it on repeat like a good old tear-jerking movie. We play audio clips of all the negative, soul-crushing, demeaning comments that were ever made toward us, over and over like a scratched record on autoplay. To take charge of our mindset in these situations, we must speak louder than the sound of defeat, louder than the sound of the tidal wave of our life crashing in around us, louder than the sound of our tears of agony and hurt, and louder than the sound of the Enemy's voice in our ears.

We must shout from the rooftops how awesome and amazing we are, declaring out loud to ourselves and everyone around us how fantastically gorgeous, radiantly beautiful, loved, accepted, and totally and completely awesome we are in every way, regardless of what the diagnosis or the bullies say! Whatever way you choose to express your radiant awesomeness, you must make sure you drown out the sound and feeling of defeat, and continue doing so, until you feel the truth of what you are shouting going through every cell of your body, flooding your heart with hope and joy for a beautiful new day. Every moment of every day has the potential to make us or break us. It is up to us to choose how we respond.

Lightbulb Moments to Build Audacity

1. Names can hurt you only if you give them power over you.

2. Choose to see yourself from the perspective of your heart, not your tainted experiences.

3. Do not be bothered by the opinions of people from whom you would not ask life-changing advice.

Audacious Actions to Live Well on Purpose

1. Decide today that you are amazing. Journal five key attributes that you know to be true about yourself. Start each with, "I am _____." Post your " I am" statements on a mirror and speak these life-giving attributes out loud to yourself every morning and night before you go to bed.

2. Replace each negative thought that you have about yourself or your situation with three positive things instead. When you catch yourself in "stinking thinking," immediately, no matter where you are, say out loud, "What I meant to say was _____," turning the negative comments into positive, life-giving, hope-filled comments instead.

3. The next time you have the urge to have a dark corner pity party, resist the temptation to hide away and ask your spouse or a close friend to share with you what they feel your top five strengths or attributes are. Thank them for sharing with you, and then journal what they say. Pray or meditate on these truths about who you are and how others who care about you see you.

CHAPTER 8

I Love Me, I Love Me Not: We Are All Beautiful

ALL MY LIFE I had been a very confident, capable, strong, poised, and assertive woman. My presence in a room would cause heads to turn. People wanted to speak with me and be my friend. But something happened to my soul along the way that caused this confidence to shift. My soul felt stepped on, cursed, and pressed on every side. Strangers called me names in public. People treated me as less than them due to my different abilities, pushing past me to get into buildings before me and then closing the door in my face rather than holding it open for me. Some cursed at me and insulted me because of how slowly I limped along. Others threw snide remarks at me in the grocery store checkout lane or honked their horns and gestured rudely at me because of how long it took me to get in my minivan when they were waiting for my parking space.

It was obvious that my physical limitations were the catalyst for their comments and actions, yet strangely, no one asked if I needed help. Not at the grocery store, not at the hospital, not at church. Not anywhere. People seemed to either avoid me, insult me, or mock me. Those incidents caused me to start experiencing huge insecurities about how I looked in other people's eyes. At that point in my life, I was not living beyond my diagnosis. I had a foot in both worlds: the woe-is-me world and the world of faith and hope. I was playing the victim in life, not thriving as a victorious overcomer. I knew about faith, but I didn't know faith as a way of life. I

I knew about faith, but I didn't know faith as a way of life.

looked for approval from others rather than finding it within myself and from God. Since people were no longer approving of the way I looked or moved, I struggled with my value as a woman, wife, and mother. I started going out of my way to limit the amount of time that people could see me standing or walking. I avoided situations where I would have to stand or walk long distances. I shopped only in small stores where the parking was right by the door. I would even circle the block until a parking spot right in front of the store opened up so that I would have the least possibility of being seen or embarrassed in any way.

The day I realized that people no longer saw me as "normal" was devastating for me. Have you ever had the experience when you haven't seen someone for a while, and you notice all kinds of changes with them such as their hair, skin, or weight fluctuations? We even sense a change in their energy or mood. We constantly look at ourselves in the mirror but don't often notice the small changes in our physical appearance because these changes happen so slowly. Even more astonishing is when people lose mobility. It is so gradual that they wake up one day and realize they can no longer tie their shoes, look over their shoulder, or pick up a penny off the ground. My posture was no longer tall and erect, and I stood awkwardly in a way that made it obvious that something was wrong with my body.

A few years before Dennis had prayed for me, I was in the middle of a two-year Bible teachers' training course with a very lively elderly instructor, Bert. I arrived a little bit early one day and was the first person in the class. Bert came in, and he and I started chatting. Out of the blue, he paused, looked at me intently, and said, "Can I ask you something?"

"Sure," I said.

"I don't want you to take this the wrong way. You are a very beautiful woman—stunning, actually. When I look at you from here up (as he motioned from his chest to the top of his head), you look totally normal. But at the end of the class when you get up, it takes my breath away. You do not stand or walk like normal people. There is something wrong with you. Do you mind me asking what has happened to you? Why are you bent over like that? Why do you walk with a limp?"

At first, I was a bit stunned that he would even go there. I couldn't believe he would ask me that. Then I was totally crushed as I realized that other people could see the crippling of my body, that it was no longer just me feeling pain in and of myself, but there had been a tangible shift in my outward appearance, and it was noticeable. I told him about the ankylosing spondylitis and what was happening in my body. It upset him greatly. He collapsed into his chair with a look of sadness and perplexity as I spoke.

"But you are so young," he finally said, "and you have four children." By then the rest of the class had started to gather, and he encouraged me to stay strong and to live every day to the fullest. "I'm sorry that you are going through this," Bert said. "I wish there was more that I could do. I feel lucky to have my health at 74. Here I am snowboarding, and you can hardly walk."

After that conversation with Bert, I became very self-conscious about the way that I stood, walked, and moved. He hadn't offended me; he was genuinely concerned about what was happening in my body. I became self-conscious because I realized other people were noticing that I was different from them, even though I had tried hard to minimize my deformities and not draw attention to myself. I think I may have inadvertently intensified the spotlight onto myself even more by scurrying along with my head down, walking as quickly as possible, hoping not to be noticed and trying not to make eye contact with anyone. Not only did I not feel beautiful or attractive, I felt hideous and grotesque to the very core of my being.

When I lamented about my disapproval of how I looked, my Mr. Wonderful would tell me that I was beautiful, but I would roll my eyes at him and blow him off. I really wanted to believe him, but by this point I was so discouraged about how my body looked that nothing he said could convince me that I was still beautiful. I mean, I could not even wear my sexy stilettos anymore. I didn't understand how my husband did not see how ugly and disfigured my body had become. He could not see what I saw because he did not see me for my outward appearance. This was partly because my disfigurement happened slowly and this was my "new normal," but really it was because he saw my heart and my soul. He saw the real me. He saw my true beauty.

It was I who had lost sight of who I was. I had been measuring myself only by my outward appearance. No wonder people picked on me—I was picking on myself. Bullying is the ultimate form of weakness of mind and mouth. Intimidation and harassment of another person is despicable, yet how often do we bully ourselves? Allowing ourselves and others to get away with bullying,

It was I who had lost sight of who I was.

especially when we see it happening and say nothing, is the ultimate sign of disrespect. Standing up for one another and ourselves is one of the most courageous things we can do. It is a sign of love.

We Are All Equal

When I was a young teen, my parents would take us to volunteer at an annual concert that was held for mentally and physically handicapped and disabled adults. At first, I found the whole event unsettling and would cry about going. Some people drooled and groaned, and some yelled and screamed or babbled nonsensically. Sometimes people would try to grab me because they needed something, and it scared me. I did not understand why they couldn't talk properly or why they acted strangely. Their faces were often distorted in some way, and their bodies were deformed and misshapen. Many had medical tubes coming out of their bodies and were hooked up to machines and came in on hospital beds. Interestingly, the more I volunteered, the more I enjoyed going. I discovered there was nothing wrong with any of these people; this was how they were made.

I made connections with some of the annual attendees and looked forward to seeing them every year. I learned how to connect with them on a deep level even when they could not speak to me. I would tell them stories, make them laugh, or hold their hand when I saw they were sad or scared. It was painful to watch those beautiful people struggle to talk, walk, and even breathe. I wondered what their life was like, not what it had been like, and how difficult it must be. I felt sad for them and wanted to help them as much as possible. Volunteering taught me a lot about human nature.

During the concerts I would sit at the back and watch all the amazing differently abled people. I mused at how they were regular people, just like me. They loved the music and would try to clap or sing along. I watched how they laughed at the same things I laughed at. I will never forget the young man who had enjoyed one of the performances so much that he stood up and started clapping, laughing, and yelling wildly. What he was saying with his voice was incomprehensible, but what he was saying with his actions could not have been misinterpreted. He had enjoyed that performance, and he was letting everyone know.

Looking back, I was happy that my parents made me go. It taught me a lot about a special group of people who most of the world didn't know existed. They can teach us a lot about the simplicity of life and enjoying each moment to the fullest. People are people. We all have the same basic human needs. No one is more valuable. No one is less valuable. We are all created equal.

Through volunteering, I learned the finer skills of opening a door for another person, saying hello to a stranger, giving a handshake or a hug. I also learned how to look someone in the eyes and let them know they are valued and loved without speaking. I learned that communication goes well beyond words, that every person is unique and special, and that every person has something to give to the world around them—everyone.

Differently Abled

Even knowing all of this, somehow it felt different when I was in the differently abled category. I knew these things for other people, but I did not know how to thrive in the world as differently abled myself. Friends and family just assumed that I could do everything the same as them and as fast as them. Waking up daily with extreme brain fog, stiffness, and pain was never a fun way to wake up. I could not just pop out of bed; it took me a long time to get going. I moved slowly and carefully. I needed more time to get tasks done. I could not stand up straight. I could not easily reach down and pick up something I had dropped. I could not make sudden movements. I looked awkward because I was. It wasn't any less awkward for me than for those watching me. I desperately wanted to be normal, but I wasn't. I found it hard to look in a mirror and accept myself when I felt so ugly in a body that was unrecognizable to me. *I love me, I love me not* was a constant exchange in my mind.

One of my best friends often told me to get over myself, that my life was not that hard and that many people had it way worse than me. She would remind me about all the people in the world who were born with no arms or legs, how they were doing amazing things and living totally normal lives. Although I agreed with her because they certainly were doing remarkable things, such as painting beautiful pictures with their feet or winning gold medals, the difference between me and them in my mind was that they did not know what it was like to be born "normal." This had always been their life, right out of the womb. It was normal for them.

I felt horrible for saying this, especially given my volunteer experiences, because I had that small glimpse into how challenging the lives of differently abled people were. But at that point I was focused on what was wrong with my life rather than creating my own beautiful life despite the diagnosis and changes to my body. I was so hyper-focused on trying to hide what was happening in my body and appear normal at all costs that I missed out on living. I found it hard to look in a mirror and accept myself when I felt so ugly in a body that was unrecognizable to me. I held myself captive by negative, defeatist thoughts. I was holding on for dear life rather than experiencing

I was focused on what was wrong with my life rather than creating my own beautiful life.

life to the fullest as that differently abled man had taught me so many years ago.

As I watched my ability to live with grace and ease gradually disappear, I often reflected on what Dr. Susan had spoken over me. I worried that I would not find a way to stay out of that wheelchair. This concern pushed me to try numerous supplements and natural treatments to regain my health, no matter the cost. I drew a line in the sand and decided that enough was enough. I would never give up—not ever. There was no way in hell I was ever getting in that wheelchair. I did not care what it took.

It grieves me to see how the world treats differently abled people with disrespect and disdain. Some people like to squash disabled people like bugs with their words and actions. I was discovering this firsthand for myself. Shortly after my first hip replacement in 2015, I was walking into a mall. I was very shaky, using a cane, and walking very slowly. A woman who was walking toward me locked her eyes with mine and stared me down. She never averted her gaze and made it clear that she was not moving out of my way. She kept walking straight toward me as if she were playing chicken with me. I could not believe that she was trying to intimidate me like this, so I kept walking, shifting my glance to the side to get out of her dead-lock stare, yet she kept walking straight at me. When she was within two steps of me, I nearly tripped as I moved out of her way because I was certain that she would run right into me and knock the cane out from under me. What gall she had to confront a differently abled person and try to make me move out of her way.

While people's offensive attitudes toward disabled people were evident to me, I will confess that walking with the cane made my life a little bit easier. When I was using a cane, people could see that I was mobility-challenged. I did not have to explain why I walked that way or stood that way. Nobody asked me why I had a cane or why I walked the way I walked. The cane was like an outward flashing sign that read, "Hey, I am different than you, please respect me." The cane seemed to speak for itself. It made being out in public easier.

Assumptions Can Lead to Misunderstandings

One Sunday afternoon, I was trying on bras at a department store. One of the senior fitters, a very put together, prim and proper, impeccably dressed English woman, was helping me. At one point she remarked that she really liked the fit of the bra I had on but it would look a whole lot better if I would just stand up straight. I turned around to face her and said, "I can't stand up straight. I have an autoimmune disease that has fused my spine together. This is as straight as I get." A look of horror came across her face.

"I am so sorry, I didn't know. Please forgive me; that was so rude," she stammered, totally embarrassed. I felt bad for her. It looked as if she was trying to find the nearest rock to crawl under. She felt so guilty about what she had said that she ramped up her already amazing service and gave me a huge discount as well.

People assume a lot of things about a person based on how they look. We could alleviate many misunderstandings and hurt feelings if only we asked better questions and had a little more compassion for those around us. If we seek to understand the people around us rather than tease them or crush them because they talk, look, or act differently than us, we would find more pleasure and joy in our daily interactions, and those around us would feel more supported, valued, and loved.

Be a life-giver to those you meet. By showing love and acceptance through your words and actions, you can brighten someone's day and encourage them to love and accept themselves. This is one of the sweetest ways for your inner beauty to shine.

Lightbulb Moments to Build Audacity

1. You are beautifully and wonderfully made. You are unique; there has never been nor will there ever be anyone exactly like you. You do not need to look like or walk like anyone else. Be the best version of you, and totally rock it out because everyone else is already taken.

2. It doesn't matter what people say about you or how they look at you. If you can look in the mirror at the end of the day and tell yourself that you accept and love yourself, that is all that matters.

3. Life is too short to be held hostage by what people say, don't say, do, or don't do. We are responsible for the meanings we give to our experiences. Choose better meanings and live with more peace and joy.

Audacious Actions to Live Well on Purpose

1. Stand in front of a full-length mirror, totally undressed. Ask God to reveal to you why He loves you so much. Ask Him to help you love every inch of your beautiful body. First look yourself in the eyes and say that you love your- self. Mean it with every fiber of your being. Gaze on the rest of your body, marveling over the details of your shoul- ders, hands, belly button, and thighs, whatever strikes you the most about your features. Maybe you marvel at how strong your shoulders are and how many people you have comforted as they cried on them, or how beautiful your breasts are and how they brought life to your babies as you nursed them. Perhaps you are thankful for the surgery scar because you have a second opportunity to live well. Look at your body and give thanks and gratitude for every cell. Do not rush through this exercise. Repeat as needed if thoughts of unworthiness or unattractiveness creep into your mind.

2. Practice walking with confidence. Take long, slow strides with a smile on your face and your chin lifted high. If you pass a mirror or storefront window, admire yourself, smile, flip your hair, or put on some lipstick. Make eye contact and say hello to those you meet. Notice how it makes you feel to move this way and radiate confidence.

3. Get a makeover from a professional makeup artist to show you how to enhance your natural beauty and features. Sometimes the right lipstick can make all the difference and put a little pep in your step. Not into makeup? Get a professional bra fitting. You may be surprised to find you have been wearing the wrong size bra for years. Proper support can make a huge difference in your silhouette.

PART 2

Your
Power

CHAPTER 9

Sometimes God Works in Mysterious Ways

I WAS WORKING extensively with prayer, diet, natural therapies, and supplementation, and the AS was in "remission." I was mostly pain-free, but there was an increasing issue with my right hip. It was locking into place and getting very stiff, making putting on my shoes or taking long walks challenging.

It was winter and I was desperately trying to get my boots on. My body was not cooperating with me. I couldn't get my hip into the right position to get my boot on. Rather than getting a different pair of shoes, or asking for help, I kept trying to get on the boots I wanted to wear. We were late for church, and the kids were already waiting in the van. Scott stood there patiently, watching me struggle as my emotions raced toward having a full meltdown. Finally, in tears, I asked him to please put my boot on. Without a word, my Mr. Wonderful bent down and put my boot on.

"Thank you," I said, looking at him with shame and embarrassment through my tears.

"I love you," he replied as he kissed me on the forehead, and we walked out the door.

Why had I not asked him to help me put my boot on fifteen minutes earlier? Why was I so stubborn? Why was it so difficult for me to ask for help?

The Power of Asking for Help

Growing up as the tough girl of a big family, I never asked for help. I didn't want to be called a sissy. I was tough, and I would prove it. "Watch me" was my motto. But today my stubbornness and pride had gotten in the way, making a simple task a difficult and upsetting challenge.

My perseverance and grit had taken me far in my wellness journey, but I needed to learn that asking for help was not a sign of weakness, nor did it exclude me from being a powerful, self-sufficient woman. Asking for help is totally audacious. It can make our lives so much easier and less stressful. Asking for help shows that we know our limits. It decreases frustration, strengthens our relationships with others, and increases pleasure through service.

A few years later, in the summer of 2014, my oldest

Asking for help is totally audacious.

daughter and I went on a two-week cruise to de-stress. We had a fantastic time together touring the Caribbean, shopping, eating great food, and getting amazing tans. Ten days into the vacation, my body really started feeling the exhaustion from the heat, the miles of walking, and carrying backpacks and heavy bags. My right hip was in agony. I was limping badly. I did not want to ruin our trip, so I dug deep and kept going on our scheduled tours through gritted teeth.

By the time we were on our way home, I was in rough shape. I could barely stand, never mind walk. I had really done a number on my back and hip, and I could not wait to get home to my chiropractor. The flight home was a welcome relief as I knew that I would be able to sleep in my own bed, see my chiropractor, Dr. David, and be back to new in a day or two.

When the plane landed in Canada, it hit the runway with such force that my body jarred in my seat and my pelvis locked as searing pain radiated in my pelvis and hips, up my spine, and into my neck. I could not breathe; my whole body was spasming and in excruciating pain. Normally in this situation I would sit, breathe, pray, and try to relax to allow my body to calm down. I waited to deboard until the plane had totally unloaded, but my pelvis was still in full spasm. The pain was unbearable as I tried to stand. My body did not want me to put any weight on my right side, but we had to get off the plane and clear customs. I told my daughter that she would have to carry everything. When I say everything, I mean everything. She had our carry-ons, purses, and backpacks, and still we had to collect our luggage from the carousel in order to go through customs. She looked like a pack mule and worked up a sweat as she carried all our belongings and held me up while we made our way through the airport.

At one point we needed to go up an escalator. My pelvis was still spasming, and I was holding on to the railing for dear life. Suddenly I felt a heavy thud on my back and felt excruciating pain in my back and my hips as a very large suitcase came out of nowhere and landed on my back, sending my whole body into spasms. Gasping for breath, I saw that the top of the escalator was coming. Fear struck me. I had no idea how I was going to be able to step off the escalator. My entire body was spasming, my pelvis was rocking back and forth, I couldn't breathe, I couldn't move, and I was totally freaking out. In a sheer force of will, I launched myself forward at the top of the escalator, screaming in pain and hoping that I would not collapse on the ground in the process. Thankfully, I didn't fall getting off the escalator, but we still had to walk about half a mile to our boarding gate and I was in more pain than before.

Gripping my thighs for support, with all the energy and strength that I had, I started moving toward the customs area with tears streaming down my face. All I wanted to do was sit down, but I knew that I could not stop, or we would miss our final flight. When the customs officer saw me struggling to walk, she waved me over to the handicap lane, saying that it would be easier for me because there was no line. She did not realize that it was about three times farther to walk. By the time we got up to the customs desk, I was a total mess. I was huffing and puffing, tears were streaming down my face, and I was in absolute agony.

The customs officer looked at me with great concern and asked my daughter if I was okay. My daughter told her that I was injured, but that I would be okay.

The customs officer looked at me intently and then said, "You know we have wheelchairs for people like you." Those words pierced me. *People like me? How dare she*, I thought. With every ounce of strength I had, I pulled myself together and looked her dead in the eye.

"People like me? You do not know anything about me. I was supposed to be in a wheelchair for the rest of my life by the time I was thirty-five. I did not get in it then, and I won't get in it now. I will never get in that wheelchair. Never," I snarled at her with hostility and rage. The customs officer looked at me like I was a raving lunatic. She looked at my daughter, stamped our passports, and waved us through without asking any further questions.

By this time, I seriously thought I was going to die from pain. All I could do was put one foot in front of the other, clench my teeth, grip my legs, and pray that we would make it to the gate on time. My daughter was exhausted from doing her best to juggle everything, including me. At long last, we made it to the gate. I had time to go to the washroom to deal with this pain the only way I knew how. I went into a stall and commanded the pain to leave my body in the name of Jesus Christ. I told the devil to back off and get away from me, stamped my foot hard into the pavement, and told my body to line up with the Word of God. I did this out loud, over and over again, until all the pain was totally gone. We boarded the aircraft, had a great flight home, and I left the airport walking, free of pain.

It was not all rosy after that. After being away for two weeks from my Mr. Wonderful, that night we made passionate love and fell asleep in each other's arms. When I woke up the next day, my hip had firmly locked into place. I had extreme pain down the right side of my body. Even moving my pinky toe caused excruciating pain. I went to Dr. David, who had always been able to get me back on track, three times a week for months. Nothing was shifting. The chiropractic treatments would help minimally for a few hours, maybe a day, and then I would be right back to where I had been. Things seemed to be getting worse. I prayed many times a day. The prayer team and everyone I knew were praying for me. The pain persisted. I didn't understand why my regular fixes were not helping.

In December, after six months of suffering, I called my homeopath and told him what had happened. He advised me to see my family doctor and get some X-rays, blood work, and an ultrasound-guided cortisone injection to try and reduce the pain. It had been about five years since I had last seen my doctor because every complaint I had was dismissed due to the AS. I had been told many times that I didn't have hip problems, it was my spine from the AS. She was alarmed at the extreme limits to my mobility and high level of pain. She readily agreed to the X-rays and the blood work. In a few days, I was back in her office discussing the potential need for not one, but two emergency hip replacements. I was a bit shocked and really did not believe her assessment of the situation. She sent in a request to the Joint Assessment Clinic. All I could do was wait. Weeks went by and I heard nothing. It felt like I was back at the beginning of the diagnosis. I was having problems sitting, and once I was seated, I was having problems standing. My hip seemed to be completely locked in place. Even getting into bed was nearly impossible. I couldn't lift my leg without literally picking it up and moving it. My body would seize in agony. I was paralyzed, half in bed and half out, waiting for the spasms to stop so I could sleep. The only thing that my Mr. Wonderful could do was watch me writhe in pain. There was nothing he could do to help. There was nothing he could do to take away the pain except kiss me, hold me, and pray.

Every day I got up, showered, dressed, did my hair, put my makeup on, and went to work. By the time I had gotten ready in the morning, I was already exhausted from the pain. But I never gave up. Not once did I lie in bed or call in sick. I simply got up, showed up, and did my best to serve my clients in my natural wellness clinic. Every. Single. Day. I even maintained my schedule teaching nutrition and blood analysis.

Despite the pain I was in, I had a mission to help people live well. I knew that our bodies are designed to heal. I knew that my clients didn't have to suffer, and I wanted to be there for them to show them the way back to health. I needed to be there for them. Serving my clients helped to shift my focus

We must learn to challenge our minds to think better, act better, feel better, and see better.

away from me and on to them to find solutions for their problems and be a light in their darkness, which brought me pleasure.

When we are consumed by pain and fatigue in our own body, shifting our focus outside of ourselves is key. Pain can be consuming, so much so that it is all we see, all we think, and all we feel. Life is much more than the pain we are feeling at any current moment. We must learn to challenge our minds to think better, act better, feel better, and see better.

When I was with my clients, my focus was on them, not my pain. I could still feel the pain if I moved the wrong way, and when I got up to show them out, the pain was overwhelming. I needed a minute or two to convince my body that it could take a step without collapsing, but I persisted.

Despite the pain, I showed up every day. Not just in survival mode, but in thriving mode. I didn't stop ministering, leading worship, or being a mom and a wife. I worked my gardens and tended to my chickens, sheep, goat, and donkey. I got the groceries, made the meals, and cleaned the house, all with excruciating pain, because these things give me life and prove to me that life is worth living. Being in nature with my gardens and animals is a connection point with God. It grounds me, and my stress drifts away. Having my hands in the dirt is a small grace from God. The dirt is where all my problems and pain disappear and where all that I hear is the Father's heartbeat and His love song being sung over me. Gardening is a great way for me to refocus. When we get creative, it occupies our minds and we focus less on our challenges or pain. Finding a creative outlet feeds our soul and brings balance into our day.

It would have been easier to lie in bed and hope for the next best medication. But audacious living is not about the easy way. We will never find healing lying in our bed. I've built my life on persistence and sheer grit. There was no way in hell I was giving up now. There was a way, and I would find it.

Overwhelmed by pain and desperation to find out what was wrong with me, I called the Joint Assessment Clinic to see where I was in the queue. I explained to the nurse I was in a lot of pain and that I was having problems sitting, standing, and walking. It was even challenging going to the washroom. At first the nurse was patronizing. She told me that just because I was in pain, it didn't mean I needed a hip replacement. I told her that I didn't want a hip replacement, I just wanted to know why I was in so much pain and what I could do to stop it. She told me to be patient while she tried to find my file and that it would take a while. Less than two minutes later, she was back on the phone, telling me that I had a medical emergency and that they would see me in two days.

I felt relieved that I was finally going to get some answers. Two days later at my appointment, a nurse practitioner assessed the status of my hips to see if I qualified for surgery. She started with my left hip because I was not having any pain in it. She thought I still had a couple of years left on it and moved on to assess my right hip.

I will never forget the look that came across her face when she picked up my right leg and moved it slightly to the right. She looked at me with horror in her eyes and put my leg right back on the table.

"I am not touching that," she said. "Congratulations, you need a hip replacement. I have never seen anything this bad. I am going to do you the biggest favor of your life. I happen to know that the best surgeon in Ottawa has a cancellation for next week, and you're going to be getting that appointment." She picked up the phone and booked the appointment right there. I thought she was totally overreacting. I mean, she was a nurse practitioner, not the doctor, and she had hardly even touched me. What could she really know? I wanted to know what the orthopedic surgeon would say. I was confident that he would say I was fine and just give me a cortisone shot. The following week I went back to the hospital to meet with the surgeon. This time I took my Mr. Wonderful with me, hoping he would tell the doctor that I really did not need a hip replacement.

As we went into the room, the surgeon was looking at my X-rays. "I see that you are looking at my beautiful pictures," I chuckled.

The orthopedic surgeon turned around with a look of alarm on his face and said to me sternly, "These are not beautiful. This is a nightmare. I have never seen anything worse in my entire career. You need a hip replacement. Where were you ten years ago?"

"You and I both know that ten years ago you would have

never replaced my hip. I would have been too young," I retorted.

"I absolutely would have. This is a disaster. Mrs. Harris, I don't know what I can do to help you. I know I can replace your hip and that you will no longer be in pain. But I do not know if you will ever be able to walk again. In fact, I don't even know how you walked in here. Looking at your X-rays, it is physically impossible for you to be walking."

That was news to me, so I said, "Nobody told me that I couldn't walk, so I just do. I have no choice."

"Sure," he said, "if that's what you call walking," referring to how I threw the whole right side of my body forward to walk. "We need to schedule surgery immediately. I will be doing the surgery myself. No residents or interns will be assisting me. I can't afford for anything to be screwed up. You are very young, and I want to give you the best life that I can."

Because of a family history of anaphylaxis to anesthesia, and extremely low hemoglobin due to the massive levels of inflammation, I was awake for the whole hip replacement with only a spinal anesthetic. As I was being prepped for the spinal anesthetic, a beautiful man with the kindest eyes came up to me, saying that he was here to support me while they were putting in the epidural. He invited me to lean on his shoulder so he could hold me up. I have no idea where he came from. He was not in the operating suite before, and he was not in the room after. There was something about him that was so calming and peaceful. I looked into his eyes and felt love looking back at me. I was drawn to him. "Do you know Jesus?" I asked.

"Yes, I do," he said, and with that I melted into his shoulder and all of my fear and anxiety disappeared. Going into the surgery, I had been distraught for days. I had spent lots of time crying, telling my Mr. Wonderful that I probably would not go through with the surgery, that Jesus was enough and that He would heal me before the surgery date. I prayed for healing. I prayed that when the surgeon cut into my hip, he would find a perfectly healthy hip and would be amazed and declare it a miracle.

The morning of the surgery, I woke up and realized I was still in pain. I knew I had to have my hip replaced. I was disappointed but believed a miracle would happen at any moment so that I would not have to go through with the surgery. I spent a long time taking a hot bath, listening to worship music, and shifting my mindset. I thanked God for keeping me safe. I thanked Him for my family and my Mr. Wonderful. I asked Him for peace and to help me breathe. By the time I got downstairs to leave for the hospital, I was upbeat and peaceful and calm. As we drove to the hospital, I could tell that my Mr. Wonderful was wondering why I was not completely freaking out, crying, and hyperventilating. Why was I just sitting there chatting away, completely calm? I could tell he wanted to ask me but was afraid in case it set me off. He was waiting for me to completely lose it, yet that moment would never come. As I was being prepped for surgery, I was making jokes with him and the nurse. With the ridiculous cap on my head, without makeup, and draped in an ugly gown, I asked him to take some fun pictures of me.

Finally, he said, "I can't believe that you're not freaking out. Are you okay?"

"What's there to freak out about?" I smiled. "Jesus has me. He will heal me; it is well."

Prayer is a underutilized weapon that disarms anxiety and fear. Spending time in daily prayer can elevate our mood as we shift our focus on God, bringing peace and hope to our situation.

I prayed until the very last moment that they would find nothing wrong with my hip when they opened me up. That didn't happen. The doctor opened me up and proceeded with the surgery. It was strange hearing all the sounds and seeing all the things in the operating suite. To pass the time, I chatted, prayed, and sang worship songs out loud. At one point I made a joke asking the surgeon if he could do a little liposuction while he was down there. I thought I was hilarious. Unfortunately, he did not. Secretly, though, I think this is when he and I became friends. The nurse laughed and told me I had nothing down there to liposuction. I told her she was blind and needed to look harder. We both laughed. The surgery was very compli-cated, and the laughter cut the tension in the room. It seemed to help everyone relax.

Until I heard the sound of the saw. I stopped singing for a moment, wondering what that sound was. When I realized they were literally sawing the head of my femur off, I needed a distraction really fast. This sound was more than slightly disturbing, so I began to sing louder to drown out the noise of the saw. A few minutes later I could hear a dripping noise. It was dripping faster and faster. The pinging sound of my blood dripping into the stainless steel basin sent me into a bit of panic as I realized that I was hemorrhaging. The operating suite went quiet. I could feel the mood shift back to serious. I was all out of jokes, so I ramped up my prayers. A few moments later my whole body was being jarred by the force of the doctor pounding my new hip into place. It sounded like a steel mallet pounding in railroad ties. It vibrated throughout my entire body, sending shock waves up and down my spine. I found myself clenching my abs to try to buffer the blows. I asked the anesthetist to bump up the juice.

In the recovery room, the spinal anesthetic was wearing off, and I was amazed that I had no pain. I sat propped up on pillows, looking at my toes popping out of the covers at the end of the bed. I was weeping with joy as I looked at my feet, which were perfectly positioned and pointing up looking back at me. For years before the surgery, I could not physically force my foot to be perpendicular to the bed. It was always twisted outward, and there had been nothing I could do to straighten it. Seeing it perpendicular, straight as a board, without pain, was totally amazing, and the fact that I was alive was even better.

The morning after my surgery, the physiotherapist came to the room to start my rehabilitation exercises. The first thing she did was get me up to start walking. We were about halfway around the nursing station when she finally stopped me and asked why I was walking like that.

"Like what?" I asked her.

"Why are you not lifting your leg when you walk?" she asked.

Confused, I looked at her and said, "I have no idea what you're talking about."

"When you walk, you're supposed to lift your leg and bend your knee, but you are basically dragging your leg behind you."

"I don't know what you are saying," I said. "I hear you speaking English words but my brain does not understand what you are saying." She thought it was strange and that it was a little post-surgical disconnect or fatigue from the anesthetic. She had her assistant help me by tapping my leg and calling out, "Lift your leg, bend your knee, lift your leg, bend your knee," every time my right foot struck the ground.

The physiotherapist wanted to show me some exercises that could be done on the bed to strengthen the muscles around my hips. The very first exercise seemed simple enough. I was lying on my back with my legs straight out in front of me, and all I needed to do was take my right leg and move it out to the side as far as I could. My brain told my leg to move. Nothing happened. I asked the physiotherapist how to do it. She looked at me oddly and said, "It doesn't matter how you do it, just do it. Just move your leg out to the right." I tried again. My brain told my leg to move out to the right. Again, nothing happened. My leg didn't move. My foot didn't move. My toes didn't move. My foot just sat there all perpendicular and pretty, looking back at me.

Frustrated, I said to the physiotherapist, "I would love to be able to do what you're asking me, but I don't know how, so if you could tell me that would be great."

Annoyed, she snapped at me and said, "It doesn't matter

how you do it; just move it."

"There seems to be a miscommunication. Earlier you brought me some pamphlets on how to recover after breaking a hip. I didn't break my hip. My hip was fused into the socket because I have ankylosing spondylitis. I had a full hip replacement. For the past few years, I haven't been able to move this leg at all unless I picked it up and physically moved it. So if you could tell me how to move my leg, I would really appreciate it," I explained.

"Oh!" she exclaimed. "You can't move your leg!"

I looked at her and laughed. I twirled my finger in the air, saying, "Ding, ding, ding! You are correct, you are the winner! I can't move my leg, but if you can tell me how to do it, that would be awesome. I would love to do it." She said something about sensory motor amnesia and that it would take time. She showed my Mr. Wonderful how to do the movements for me to start engaging the brain to reconnect. It was a bit of a gong show because he was afraid of hurting me, and I was also afraid that he would hurt me, but we did it together. Sometimes doing it afraid is the only way to make it happen.

My Mr. Wonderful was a champion. He would get so excited when he saw even little improvements. The first time I moved my leg on my own, Scott totally freaked out. He was elated with joy. "Did you see that? Babe, you moved your leg! You are a rock star!" he shouted, beaming with pride. Even though I had moved my leg only about an inch, he celebrated like it was a momentous achievement, because it was.

In the following weeks I spent time walking daily and

doing the hip-strengthening exercises. When we were out for a walk or getting ready to climb up the stairs at the end of the day, I would have this strange brain meltdown. I would freeze like a statue and go into panic mode. I'd look at my Mr. Wonderful with what he said was total panic in my eyes and ask him what we were doing. He would just smile and say we were going for a walk and to watch him. Then he would go in front of me and walk at a slow pace, shouting at me over his shoulder, "Lift your leg, bend your knee, lift your leg, bend your knee." This went on daily for months. I had a cane, so I was supported and wasn't going to fall, but it was freaky that my brain would just turn off and forget what I was doing. The surgeon thought this was due to exhaustion from trying to learn how to use my hip. He thought my brain was shutting off from being overwhelmed and that it should get better over time. Except it wasn't getting better. It was happening daily.

Three months later, I was back at work. I still had swelling and numbness from the surgery and had to use a cane to support myself when I walked because of the disconnect from my brain, but I was pain-free and felt fantastic. I started looking for ways to heal my brain and body connection so that I could walk normally. I had heard so many phenomenal testimonies from people who had received an essential oil therapeutic technique who had regained their mobility and were pain-free that I was eager to experience this myself.

Since my Mr. Wonderful likes to fix things, when I approached him about the opportunity to take the certification course for the essential oil technique, he was all-in because it would give him a tangible way to help me.

For years I had great challenges getting onto my own bed, never mind onto a massage table. Every time I went to my chiropractor, it was hit and miss whether I would be able to get off the table. If at any point I had to lie on my abdomen, it was certain that my back would go into a spasm and lock down, and I would not be able to get off the table. Dr. David and I had developed some rescue strategies around this situation, including using the TENS machine or acupuncture to confuse my muscles so they would not freak out and spasm. But none of these tools was available for me at this training, so all I could do was trust my Mr. Wonderful and God that I would be able to get off the table and that all would be well.

I was nervous because this would be the first time that I had lain on my stomach since my surgery ten months before. I got up on the massage table and slowly lay down on my front, but I kept myself propped up with a pillow under my head and my arms tucked up under my chest because I didn't think it was possible to fully lie flat, and I didn't want to put that much pressure on my new hip. About five minutes into the technique, I felt the small of my back spasm quickly and lock. *Here we go*, I thought. *I wonder if I'll be able to get up at the end.* I didn't tell anyone what had happened. I tried to enjoy the experience, which was surprisingly relaxing, especially because I had never really enjoyed a massage. I felt euphoric. The challenge now was to get off the table. Surprisingly, I sat right up without any pain or spasming.

All my colleagues taking the course with us were all

amazed. Not only did I get right off the table, but I was walking around more erect and relaxed. The tension in my psoas and hip flexors was gone. One of my colleagues, who is a chiropractor, was watching me with curiosity, "How did you do that?" he asked. All I could say was, "Isn't this amazing?" I was standing tall and feeling fantastic after lying on my stomach for forty-five minutes on a hard massage table. Even if this were the only benefit, it was worth it. The instructor was happy for me. She encouraged my husband to do the technique on me every night to see what would happen.

The next day when my Mr. Wonderful was applying the third essential oil (tea tree) to my spine and back of my head, I felt a weird dizziness or spinning sensation. It felt like there were electric shocks firing inside my brain. "Whoa, what are you doing? What oil is that?" I questioned him.

"It's tea tree, you know that," he said.

"It's so strange. It makes my brain feel weird," I explained. After the tea tree oil was applied, I was able to relax my arms down by my side, lying flat on my front, which was a huge improvement for me. I had not lain fully on my stomach for at least eight years. At the end of the treatment, I got right off the table and walked around feeling great, the same as the day before. The third day when Scott was doing the essential oil therapeutic technique on me, the electrical shock sensation in my brain felt like explosions when he applied the tea tree oil. I asked him again what he was doing because it was so weird. My Mr. Wonderful was totally calm and continued with my session. At the end of the treatment, I was completely relaxed in every cell of my body. As I went outside for my daily walk down our long country lane, I suddenly had the sensation of what I can only describe as tumblers in a lock falling into place and being opened. I distinctly felt a click, click, click as the whole right side of my body seemed to come into alignment. It was like I was physically feeling my brain reconnecting with the muscles and ligaments on my right side and locking them into their proper place. It made me pause and stop walking—it felt so cool. After that moment, I've never had another brain meltdown. I've never had to stop walking and wonder what I was doing midstride, and my Mr. Wonderful has never again had to walk in front of me, shouting, "Lift your leg, bend your knee." From that moment on, I've been able to stay connected and walk without hesitation.

The power of pure essential oils is astounding. They are true gifts of the earth. God works in mysterious ways. I was not expecting to receive such dramatic healing from a few drops of essential oils. He created the earth and everything in it, and He said that it was good. God has provided everything that we need to thrive in life, if only we open our senses and taste and see that the answer is right in front of us. Life truly is good.

I discovered that tea tree essential oil historically has been used in French medicine to treat shock. It finally all made sense. The shock that I had experienced many years ago when I learned about the sexual abuse of my daughters impacted me in a very profound way. I wasn't able to shift my focus or bring peace to my mind or body because the emotional shock was attached to my spine. I was unable to move forward. I had become frozen in pain, suspended in a moment of time. The shock of what had happened to my daughters had shut me down, and the gift of essential oils had brought my brain back to life. This was a huge lesson about how much our emotions can impact our physical bodies. It is so important to resolve emotional traumas.

Interestingly, many people experience the same types of traumas repeatedly. The same emotions come up and attach in the same places in our bodies, causing more and more dysfunction, pain, loss of vitality, and life itself. To stop repeating these traumas, we must change the role we give ourselves in the story to a more empowering one so that we can heal.

I have no idea why God brought essential oils into my life or why healing my brain and sensory motor amnesia didn't manifest on their own. We never know what tools we will find in our search for wellness. Sometimes it's the little things that have the greatest impact.

Lightbulb Moments to Build Audacity

1. Asking for help is not a sign of weakness. It is powerful to allow others to help you in your darkest moments.

2. Refuse to be labeled. A label or a diagnosis is not your friend;

it can make your situation worse. Once you are labeled as having a chronic disease, it can be very challenging for medical personnel to see beyond the diagnosis, and not chalk everything up to the disease rather than seeing you as a whole person with other needs and concerns.

3. It is our mindset that makes or breaks us, not people, things, or situations. It is the language and meaning we give to what is happening that either deflates or elevates our life.

Audacious Actions to Live Well on Purpose

1. Learn to ask for help. The next time you are struggling physically, emotionally, or spiritually, do not be afraid or ashamed to reach out and ask for help from a true friend.

2. Try daily prayer or meditation before the most stressful time of day for you. Journal how it shifts your focus and mood.

3. Schedule an essential oil therapeutic technique with a local certified essential oil therapeutic technique practitioner to treat yourself and bring your autonomic nervous system into balance. Journal how it makes you feel.

CHAPTER 10

Charting a Path to Rehabilitation: The Power of Belief

WHEN YOUR BODY is crippled for as long as mine was, it puts up a lot of resistance to going back to a healthy, balanced, and functioning state because it has a new normal, a dysfunctional way of existing. My body became a twisted web of muscle compensations (called *recruiting*) that affected my movement and gait. Because my spine had fused itself together, exercise was challenging. My body no longer used the appropriate muscle groups to move, and that sometimes caused injury. My chiropractor once caught me trying to use my eye muscles to lift my shoulder. The body will compensate any way it can to remain functioning and mobile.

I spent many years going to various specialists, trying out different therapies to recover the range of motion I had lost. But no one seemed to be an expert on ankylosing spondylitis. They all said they could help me, but I usually ended up worse than when I had walked in the door. When I started new exercise routines, I usually ended up at my chiropractor's office multiple times a week for months with muscle spasms. I asked my doctor many times to find me a rheumatologist and a physiotherapist who specialized in advanced AS recovery, but no one seemed to do this.

People assumed that I had a bad life because of how I looked and moved. Dr. Debbie, my rheumatologist at one point, was one such person. She was always trying to get me to take biological medication, but I disagreed with her. I no longer had symptoms of active disease, and I had been in "remission" for years. Biologics turn off your immune system and increase the risk of serious infections and side effects. One day Dr. Debbie brought it up again, and I told her there was no way I would turn off my immune system or run the risk of cancer, tuberculosis, hepatitis, or death for a medication that likely wouldn't help me at all. She retorted by saying that she could treat those diseases.

"Oh, really?" I questioned. "So you are going to guarantee that if I get cancer from this medication, you can 100 percent cure me?"

"Of course not, don't be silly," she said.

"Then why would I risk taking it when the side effects are worse than what is currently going on in my body? Not to mention the medication won't unfuse my spine, so I won't walk any better than I do now."

She snapped back at me while sizing me up with her eyes. "Look at you! What quality of life could you possibly have? Taking this medication might give you a chance to live a better life."

"A better life? You know nothing about me or my life. You assume because of how I look and walk that I have a poor quality of life. Let me tell you about my quality of life. I have an amazing husband who loves me dearly. We have a fantastic marriage and sex life. I have four amazing children. I have a hobby farm; I garden. I have a wonderful job. I am part of a healing ministry where I see miraculous healings every week. Without my faith in God, I would probably be dead by now. You don't seem to know anything about my Jesus. Jesus has kept me going. He has given me hope and joy through all of this. I have an amazing life. I won't take biologics—not now, not ever! Don't ask me again," I asserted.

Dr. Debbie assumed that I didn't have a good life, but she had never asked me what I thought about my life. Her assumption was based on how I looked, not my experience. Life is more than how we look or walk. We create the life we want to live. If you want to change your experience of life, you must put in audacious effort. Everyone dies, but not everyone truly lives.

Three years earlier, when I was getting my degree in bioregulatory medicine, I had walked into the classroom and overheard a conversation between two of my colleagues. They were talking about me, my physical deformities, how limited I

Everyone dies, but not everyone truly lives.

was, and how awful that must be for me. I went up behind them, put my arms around them and said, "At least everyone can see my pain. It's written all over my body. But for you, your pain is inside. It torments you day and night. You put on a facade and wear a mask to try to convince the outside world that your life is perfect, when in fact you are hiding in your pain and wallowing in it secretly."

Startled, they looked at me, and one of my colleagues nodded and said, "Touché, Roxanne. It is all a matter of perspective, isn't it?"

"My life is no better or worse than yours. We all have horrible situations we are dealing with. The difference is that people can see there is something wrong with me, while you pretend you don't have any problems. You are not seeking your own healing because you lie to yourself saying that your suffering isn't real or that it's not as bad as mine, because no one can see that you're hurting. The difference between you and me is that I own my junk and am doing everything I can to heal myself, while you are putting on a show, portraying that your life is better than mine, when you are hurting too."

This revelation is a total game changer. We can't heal when we lie to ourselves and others about what is happening in our body and mind.

You Are the Expert of Your Own Body

I am the only one who knows my body, how I feel, and what I want. What I wanted was to be able to move my body with grace and ease. I believed it was possible—I just had to find practitioners who believed it was possible too.

I got a referral to see a rehabilitation doctor so I could regain some of my range of motion. The specialist was super casual and totally cool. He asked if he could touch my back, and as he poked around a little bit, he became pie-eyed.

"Mrs. Harris, I have never seen anything like this before. Your fascia is so tight that your entire back feels like cement. I'm sorry to tell you this, but there is nothing I can do for you. I don't have any tools in my toolbox to help you. But I can recommend an osteopath. I don't understand what they do or how they work, but you need to find yourself the best osteopath that money can buy. I am a doctor and I know the body, but they can grab your kidney and move it around, and somehow it gets rid of all your pain. I know it sounds far-fetched, but it works. That's all I've got for you. It's been a real pleasure meeting you. I hope you find some help."

I should have been disappointed. Here was another doctor telling me he couldn't help me, but I wasn't discouraged. I thanked him for his honesty, and I left excited, knowing exactly what to do next. I had a client who had been telling me about his osteopath and encouraging me to go see him. An osteopath is a doctor who takes a whole-body approach. They perform manual manipulations as well as treat the root cause of disease, including emotional traumas. I called the osteopath's office right away and was told it was a four-month wait but that I could see someone else. Since he had come highly recommended, I was willing to wait. After all, I had already been waiting years.

My appointment with the osteopath finally arrived, and I was very nervous. I had no idea what to expect. I was worried that he was going to try and manipulate something in my body and break me or cause pain.

When I arrived at the appointment, I found it strange that there were no health history questionnaires or intake forms to fill out. Faisal, the osteopath, came out and introduced himself, and then he asked me to walk ahead of him and go into the first room on my right. As I was walking, I knew he was watching me walk. I hate it when people watch me walk; it always makes me feel extra self-conscious. I tried to walk as quickly as possible to get it over with.

As Faisal walked into the room behind me, he said, "So you have a history of chronic migraines."

"You saw that from watching me walk? Very clever."

Faisal laughed and said, "How else am I going to learn about you? Watching people walk is the best way to see what's been going on in their lives and what kind of traumas and injuries they've had. It tells me a lot about them. So do you have chronic migraines?"

"Yes, I used to have them a lot, but since my son was

born, I rarely have them now."

"Oh, good for you. That's fantastic, but the imprint is still there, and we will need to fix that. You also had a blow to your head, specifically to your right cheek, when you were about two or three years old. It tilted your head off its axis, and everything you are experiencing in your body, all of the spinal curvature and fusion, has been a result of that hit to your head."

I was dumbfounded. How did he know these things from watching me walk?

"When I was two, my mom was raking the lawn and I walked behind her, and the end of the rake hit me right on my cheekbone. My face was black and blue for quite a while, and I still have the scar," I replied, pointing to the scar on my cheekbone.

"Well, then, that's a great place to start. I don't think it's going to be too complicated. In three or four treatments we will have you back on your feet feeling great," he reassured.

"In three or four treatments? I'd like to see that."

He smiled and told me to wait and see. We talked for the next half hour about my spine and hip replacements. By the time I got up on the treatment table, we had only a few minutes left in the appointment, so he said he would take it slow and not stir up too much, saying it would be very easy to go right to the source of the problem, as many other practitioners would have done, but that it would destabilize me and set me back rather than help me. I was thankful because I'd had far too many of those destabilizing treatments in the past.

Faisal put his hands on either side of my head, and I could

feel his hands lightly pressing into the sides of my head, his fingers gently manipulating the tissues. The movements were so gentle that I wondered if he were really doing anything at all. Suddenly I felt the most bizarre sensation in the middle of my brain. It was as if something deep in my brain were being rotated and flipped around.

"Oh, my, what's happening?" I said, gripping the sides of the table, trying to stop the spinning. "Something in my brain is moving."

Faisal casually said, "I'm just mobilizing your sphenoethmoidal junction. It's been jammed ever since you were hit in the head. You're going to feel a little bit strange when you get up as everything goes back to where it should be and your brain rights itself."

My sphenoethmoidal juncture? You must be crazy, I thought. *How on earth are you moving something that deep inside my brain? It's impossible.* He told me to take a deep breath in and out. He tapped me on my shoulders and told me to get up— *slowly.* As I sat up, everything in the room started shifting and moving. *What's happening?* I thought in a moment of panic. *Did he break me?* My eyes were having problems focusing. It wasn't my eyes; it was my brain. I could sense that my brain was trying to find a new center. Faisal started talking to me in his soft, gentle tone, telling me about all the things I would notice that may be different about my body and the way I moved. He said it may take up to three days to feel the full effects.

"I can already tell you what's different!" I exclaimed. I started listing everything in my body that had shifted: my breathing, my posture, the muscles in my neck and back were relaxed and not pulling to the left, my psoas was not spasming, and my balance was centered. He was very impressed by how aware I was of my body and told me to take it slow for the next forty-eight hours to give my brain a chance to reorient.

How was it possible to experience so much change when he had spent only about five minutes working on my head? There was a beautiful peace in my body. I was overjoyed at how simple this treatment had seemed and how effective it was.

After dinner, I grabbed an armful of books and some towels and started up the staircase. I was about halfway up when I realized I wasn't even using the cane that I had been using ever since my hip replacement. The cane wasn't even on the ground; it was suspended in the air, tucked in the crook of my elbow. I wasn't leaning on the banister either. Was this really happening? I was a little freaked out and started calling for Scott to come.

"What's wrong?" my Mr. Wonderful asked, nervously looking up the staircase at me.

"I just need you to watch me," I said excitedly.

"Okay, but what's wrong?" he asked again.

"I just need you to watch me walk up the stairs," I said as I turned around and continued up the rest of the stairs. When I got to the top, I spun around and looked at his stunned face.

"How did you do that?" he quizzed.

"I don't know. It was five minutes, babe. He touched my head for five minutes."

"That's amazing," my Mr. Wonderful said, beaming with

joy. I was ecstatic! The rehabilitation specialist was right. I needed an osteopath. I still had no idea what Faisal actually had done, but it was working.

I still have regular appointments with Faisal. We have thought-provoking conversations around the limits I have put on my mind and body. He reminds me to reconsider the language that I choose when discussing a challenge in my life. Changing our perspective can unravel the pain of the body and soul and help us to get out of our own way so that we can fulfill our purpose. Our life's mission can be fulfilled only when we are fully alive in who we were created to be.

Speak Life

We use language casually, almost flippantly. Rarely do we realize the power our words have on our minds and bodies, and how they shape our reality. Whether a prognosis, a traumatic event, or simply how we feel, the language we choose to use makes all the difference between deciding to live or die in that moment. Our language can make us recoil, crawling back into bed and pulling the covers over our head in isolation, devastation, and pain, or it can allow us to burst forth with passion and hope, thriving in even in the most challenging situations. Every moment, we choose whether we will participate and live or whether we will disconnect and allow our hopes, dreams, relationships, and body to die a little bit more in the dark moments that come our way.

I am more than a little tenacious. I dream the impossible because all things are possible for those who believe. There is a story in Ezekiel 37:1–10 about dry bones in the valley of death that were brought back to life by speaking the Word of God to them. For me, if God did it once, it is forever a possibility. Since God brought the bones of a whole army back to life, then surely He could do that for me too. I frequently speak to my bones and command them back to life. That is faith in action, and the power of life and death is in the tongue. Use your language to give action to your faith.

Faisal and Dr. David are integral parts of my support team. I trust them completely. They may not be specialists in AS, but they are specialists in understanding my particular body mechanics, pain, and how trauma has affected my body.

A diagnosis doesn't have to be the end of living; it can be the starting point to being audaciously alive.

My body is healing itself because I believe it will. I choose to see the possibilities and speak a better prognosis over my life. A diagnosis doesn't have to be the end of living; it can be the starting point to being audaciously alive. Audacious living is taking bold risks even if it goes against standard practice. It is the courage to stand up for yourself, your beliefs, and your dreams. It is the guts to believe in yourself to make it happen, to create your own future, and to walk boldly in faith where no woman may have gone before. It is having the moxie to say *no* and to never look back and doubt your decision. Audacity is the stance of a warrior knowing what she wants and going after it until she gets it, no matter what. It is living out your hope to create your beautiful life.

Author Max Lucado shared his thoughts on hope: "Hope is not what you'd expect; it is what you would never dream. It is a wild, improbable tale with a pinch-me-I'm-dreaming ending. . . . Hope is not a granted wish or a favour performed; no, it is far greater than that. It is a zany, unpredictable dependence on a God who loves to surprise us out of our socks and be there in the flesh to see our reaction." (For reference, see "The Thrill of Hope," Agape, https://agaperiding.org/news/the-thrill-of-hope/.)

I hope for the day that the impossible stares back at me in the mirror.

Lightbulb Moments to Build Audacity

1. You can't heal if you pretend you don't have a problem.

2. We all need a team of cheerleaders and practitioners to support us on our wellness journey. Handpick your team.

Choose practitioners who align with your vision, goals, and dreams for your life, who are willing to challenge you and push you to be all that you can be.

3. Status quo health care and placating your symptoms don't provide healing or a cure. Take bold actions to develop a wellness lifestyle.

Audacious Actions to Live Well on Purpose

1. Journal your definition of health. What is the quality of your life? Write down your vision and dreams for your health physically and emotionally.

2. Find a team of practitioners who will support you fully in your wellness goals and dreams. Do not settle for mediocre health care.

3. Journal three things you can do or stop doing, starting today, that will better support your body physically or emotionally to help it function as the precision machine that it is.

CHAPTER 11

The Power of Pussy

OPPORTUNITIES ARISE in our life that for some myste-rious reason we are drawn to, even though we are not sure why. Sometimes these opportunities challenge our thoughts, beliefs, and understanding in very painful ways. Without this stretching we would stop growing and miss out on life in some ways.

In December 2018 I was invited to a women's conference in New York to learn tools and strategies to grow my business. What I did not know was how radically this event would revo-lutionize my life.

The conference began and I was eager to learn some business breakthroughs. Or at least that is what I thought was happening, until the very first speaker used a word that startled me. *Did she actually say the p-word in her out loud voice?* Then

I heard it again, the p-word. I had never spoken that word in my entire life. It was a word I had only heard as a demoralizing, demeaning exploitation of the female gender and all things sensually and beautifully woman. The entire ballroom was businesswomen; this made no sense to me.

At the end of the second day, the host of the event announced that the next morning, anyone who wanted to learn more about how to help yourself get in touch with your inner woman, your "p-power," so that you could take charge of your business and your dreams, was invited to an unannounced session at 7:00 a.m. What?! I couldn't believe my ears. I wasn't a prude, but this was over the top. What did the p-word have to do with our business success? This conference was taking such a hard turn that I debated going home.

I called my Mr. Wonderful to ask him what to do. He encouraged me to go to the session, hoping there was some big revelation to help me in my business. I arrived at 7:02 a.m. and the door was locked. There was a note on the door that said,

Private Session Now in Progress.

No Admittance for Latecomers.

What? This is crazy, I thought. *I guess this is something I don't need to know about.* There had to be another reason why I had been inspired to come to this conference.

The morning session was buzzing, the energy was electric, and the women were giddy. Those who had attended the private session were asked to stand up. A group of women from my table stood proudly, grinning from ear to ear, giggling, beaming with joy and a radiance they hadn't had before. They seemed to be alive in a very different way. The organizers asked for testimonies, and women of all ages, races, and personalities started sharing why the earlier session was the most powerful thing they had attended in years, if not ever, and how beautiful and free they felt from tapping into their power. A middle-aged woman from my table got up and cried as she shared how utterly life-changing and transformational the session had been for her. She said she was a new woman, that she would never be the same, and that her business would explode because of learning this one thing: "The Power of Pussy."

"The Power of Pussy"

I was speechless yet intrigued. I had no grasp of what these women were talking about. I couldn't make sense of their words, their experience, or their newfound radiance. I had a belief about what pussy was, and this was not it. Each woman clearly had had a transformational experience, but I didn't exactly know what "it" was.

Throughout the conference, the speakers kept bringing up the concept of pussy in some way throughout their presentations.

The final speaker of the conference was Dr. Z, whom I admired, a lovely, godly woman with a beautiful, kind spirit. She was the main reason I had traveled to this conference. I wanted to uplevel my coaching skills and build my clinical practice as a board certified bioregulatory medicine practitioner, holistic nutritionist, and blood microscopist. I wanted to know what she had done to have become so successful because I wanted to help even more women overcome chronic disease.

"I've been really contemplating what to say to you," she said gently. "Even though I have prepared a beautiful presentation, I really feel that we have to unpack the elephant in the room and get real about pussy." My jaw dropped to the ground. I was not expecting her to go there.

She discussed the difference between how we use our feminine and masculine energies in all areas of life. She pointed out that when many women strive for success, we turn off our feminine side, thinking we need to be more assertive, serious, competitive, and driven to succeed at the cost of expressing our feminine nature of sensitivity, creativity, grace, kindness, compassion, generosity, and love. This can make us feel frustrated and puts pressure on our relationships because we aren't being our authentic selves. We miss out on the very essence of who we are when we are out of tune with our pussy, our creative center.

As women we need to access our feminine side more to be able to perform both in the business world and in life itself in a way that honors our needs to be seen, heard, and loved. When this happens, we are more creative, get more accomplished, and experience more pleasure in our day, even as a stay-at-home mom or grandmother.

Women are born to create, and when we can't create or don't make time to, it profoundly affects our mood, energy, and emotions. When a woman can't tap into her creative feminine side, her pleasure with work, relationships, and life itself starts to diminish.

Women are born to create, and when we can't create or don't make time to, it profoundly affects our mood, energy, and emotions.

I had not been creative in a long time. I had stopped doing most of the hobbies I loved so much—things that brought me pleasure, such as pottery. After my hip replacement, I couldn't spread my legs wide enough to get around my pottery wheel, and if I did manage to get close enough, being hunched over for so long put my back into spasm. So I abandoned the hobby that gave me great pleasure, and I threw myself into my career, thinking that success would bring me the pleasure I desired, but it didn't. I felt like I was missing out on life and was no longer having fun.

Many women with chronic disease stop doing the hobbies they love, including the pleasure of intimacy, because it hurts too much or they are too tired.

When we tap into our pussy, it releases our feminine side, helping us to create passion and enjoyment in every area of our life, including our work, relationships, hobbies, and health. I needed to bring my feminine creativity, passion, and joy into my soul so that life and work were fun again.

It all Came Down to Pussy

I was captivated by Dr. Z's presentation. She knew something that I didn't, and she was always radiant to prove it. I was going to get what she had. When she came off the stage, I met her in the aisle. I grabbed both of her arms, looked her in the eyes, and said, "That was one of the most challenging and interesting things I have ever heard. I was so upset when you changed your subject and started talking about pussy. I want what you have. I am going to read that book because I value what you say, and I trust you." With a huge smile, love flooded her eyes, and she said, "Do it, Roxanne. This will change everything for you."

In the parking lot of the hotel, as I was packing up my things to drive home, I downloaded the audiobook *Pussy: A Reclamation* by Regena Thomashauer. I felt naughty for reading a book on a subject that was so controversial. I'm a good girl. I'm a Christian. Why was I reading a book about pussy? What would my husband think? I was intrigued and a bit excited. Was this topic really something that would change everything for me? I listened to the book all the way home, and I was captivated as I began a journey that has impacted my life in more ways than I could ever imagine. It was a missing puzzle piece that I did not know was lost. Understanding pussy has helped me come alive in every area of my life.

The Power of Intimacy

Until that weekend in New York, I didn't understand how much my Mr. Wonderful had been trying to help me experience pleasure, especially all those years when I was limited due to pain and mobility issues. We never gave up on our intimacy. Was it always perfect? No. Did we sometimes struggle and go weeks without connecting intimately? Yes. Honestly, sometimes it just felt like it was easier not to engage so that I wouldn't feel disappointed because it didn't look or feel the way I had come to expect. It had always been very easy for me to have an orgasm, but as my spine and hip fused, it became more challenging and made me feel like I was no longer a good lover. I found myself challenging my self-worth, which made me step back and stop engaging intimately. Many times, in this state of dried-up intimacy and lack of deep connection, I found myself doubting who I was—my career, my purpose, my joy, my peace, and even my existence.

More times than I want to remember, I sank down into a less than radiant state and found myself feeling worthless and dissatisfied, storming around the house taking out my frustrations and hurt on my children, hiding from my husband, and refusing his tender embrace. I knew that the prescription I needed most was not a medication but rather to reignite the passion within my soul through connection, intimacy, togetherness, and rekindling my passion with my lover, and myself, through hobbies that fueled me and made me come alive.

When we get the emotional connection we need, the physical intimacy will follow, allowing us to reconnect to our pussy, femininity, creativity, and passion, bringing us back to life. Our pussy doesn't come with a manual. We must discover what turns us on. Having the audacity to know what gives you pleasure both in and out of the bedroom and knowing how to access it will set you free. Sexual intimacy is crucially important. It is a sacred union, offering deep emotional connection at a level that supersedes any words. Intimacy is foundational to marriage; without it, we fail to thrive.

The Power of Pleasure

Dr. Z inspired me to step way outside my comfort zone and allow my limiting beliefs about the greatly misunderstood and wrongly sexualized "pussy" to be shattered. Pussy is not about sex, but it doesn't exclude it. Pussy encapsulates the core of our essence as women. It is our pleasure bank and where we radiate from.

I realized that I was not satisfied with my success because it didn't fulfill my passions or dreams. My achievements brought fleeting moments of happiness, not pleasure.

I wasn't living a turned-on life. My pussy was muffled, and the song I was singing was utterly out of tune. I was out of tune with my purpose, my desires, and who I was. I was simply getting by.

I wasn't radiating because I wasn't pursuing pleasure in any area of my life, such as playing my guitar, gardening, or having date nights with my Mr. Wonderful. I was an unhappy workaholic distracting myself from the pain of living an unfulfilled life, hopelessly out of touch with my femininity.

It's no wonder so many businesswomen have an autoimmune disease. They are driven to achieve at the expense of creativity, fun, and pleasure. They trade projects for pleasure while missing out on the joy of living and the people they care about the most. We must shift our focus to something that will pull us toward pleasure and allows us to reexperience the passion of life.

The Power of Orgasm

Pussy, the entire female genitalia, is our creative power bank, where life is birthed, where pleasure is experienced, and where our deepest desires are brought forth. It is connected to our emotions for both pleasure and pain. The clitoris is specifically designed for a woman to experience mind-blowing sensations that help her connect deeply to her lover, herself, and her passions. It has over eight thousand nerve endings, with the sole purpose of feeling extreme pleasure.

When a woman is connected to pleasure, she disconnects from pain. Orgasms flood the body with endorphins, giving you freedom from physical and emotional pain through intimate touch. Women experience orgasm in the clitoris, not the vagina. Women can feel pleasure from penetration because the roots of the clitoris are found inside the vagina; however, they cannot achieve orgasm through penetration alone. The clitoris itself needs direct stimulation. Women with chronic pain or mobility issues may not be able to find a position that is comfortable to stimulate the clitoris during penetration, limiting her ability to climax and release those feel-good hormones. This situation requires more creativity for the woman to experience orgasmic pleasure.

> *When a woman is connected to pleasure, she disconnects from pain.*

Importantly, over 95 percent of a woman's ability to fully engage in intimacy is about her emotional connection to her lover. Without the emotional connection, a woman can't shift gears from being a mom, taxi driver, businesswoman, or chef to being a lover. When disconnected from her pleasure center, a woman can't experience or give pleasure, and without it, her focus shifts to pain; what's wrong in her life rather than what is good. No matter how worthy the calling of her job, kids, or being on the PTA, these things can never replace tapping deep into her feminine side and experiencing rapturous pleasure.

When we are in pain, we must run toward pleasure and stay connected to our creativity so that we can focus on our passions rather than allowing ourselves to be tuned in to pain and suffering. I invite you to read the Song of Songs in your Bible and see how beautiful the passion can be between two lovers and how it may help ignite your passion and creativity.

Lightbulb Moments to Build Audacity

1. It is vitally important for a woman to embrace her radiance and have a greater understanding of the function and value of her femininity.

2. Pleasure is crucial for women to tap into their passions, creativity, and femininity.

3. Limiting beliefs can limit our ability to experience pleasure in all areas of life.

Audacious Actions to Live Well on Purpose

1. Schedule a date night with your spouse or yourself to explore your body in a fun way with the sole focus of receiving pleasure. Be sure to communicate.

2. Read the Song of Songs. Write your own sensual poem about your lover and read it to them. If you don't have a lover, write a poem about yourself and read it out loud.

3. If you are struggling with self-worth, body shame, a history of abuse or dysfunctional intimacy due to chronic pain, physical limitations, or disease, find a highly recommended sex and relationship therapist for you and your spouse. Set an appointment for couples counseling as soon as possible.

CHAPTER 12

Pain, Intimacy, and Uncovering Passion Again

MR. WONDERFUL and I have a fantastic intimate relationship. We have worked extremely hard to make intimacy work for *both* of us, always making time for each other and our relationship, connecting physically and emotionally. We hold each other accountable to show up and engage fully. We have passionate encounters and a deep connection because we've worked on it. We seduced each other back into intimate connection whenever we felt there was a disconnect, no matter how small, and we never let problems go on at great lengths before enticing the other back into our arms with rapturous delight.

Through all of life's highs and lows, we stayed connected and in love. We never gave up on our relationship, because when we said "I do," we meant it. There was never a plan B. We made a choice to come together and create a family and a life together, and nothing would ever get in the way of that. Married at twenty-one, we did not know what our life would look like, but we knew that our yes to each other, before God, was an unbreakable promise, no matter what.

There were many seasons when I felt I was not the wife that my Mr. Wonderful signed up for. I was grumpy, moody, and in pain. My body couldn't bend and move the way it once had, and we had to get creative in the bedroom to try to avoid pain. Sometimes it was depressing for me not to be able to make love the way I wanted to.

One of the dark secrets that couples don't like to talk about is how chronic disease can destroy the emotional and sexual intimacy between partners. Not talking about our challenges doesn't help resolve the issues, and avoidance only makes it worse.

Society doesn't talk about sex in the context of a loving, committed relationship—and not just the act of making love but all the challenges that every couple goes through, including body shame, exhaustion, dryness, depression, fatigue, pain, lack of libido, frigidity, painful intercourse, lack of mobility, and a lack of enjoyment. Further, we have sexualized lovemaking to be all about revealing clothing, erotic fantasies, and suggestive gestures.

Intimacy goes well beyond superficial excitement, erotic

lust, and pornographic smut. Many people are not satisfied in their sexual relationships because they think that their relationship doesn't live up to what the media portrays it should be. This perceived lack leaves them more interested in experiencing butterflies in their stomach than building a loving, fulfilling, and intimate connection with their soul mate, causing many to go elsewhere searching for butterflies rather fixing their own marriage.

Butterflies are amazing, but they are not love; they are heightened arousal, excitement, or nerves. After twenty-nine years of marriage, my Mr. Wonderful still gives me butterflies when he kisses my neck, caresses my shoulders, or gazes into my eyes. He excites me because we make each other a priority and connect deeply. It is sad when people think they have fallen out of love with their spouse because they no longer feel butterflies. They don't feel butterflies because they either don't have a deep emotional connection, or they have become distracted and have become roommates rather than lovers.

Every couple has challenges with intimacy, communication, and romance at one time or another. These challenges are opportunities to improve your relationship. They are nothing to be ashamed of, but they must be addressed, especially in the context of chronic disease, pain, and fatigue. Chronic disease greatly affects our relationships and our libido, and as a friendly public service announcement, the "little blue" pill will never help the emotional struggles that come with a lack of intimacy due to pain, depression, or lack of connection.

Intimacy is vital to our wellness. Couples that engage

in frequent sexual encounters where both partners experience pleasure feel valued and loved. They have a strong marriage because of the deep emotional connection and communication that they have created through language and touch.

Intimacy is a physical, emotional, and spiritual experience. The intertwining of your bodies creates an interlocking of your spirits, and the two become one, not just for that moment but for all of time. A piece of you belongs to your beloved, and a piece of them belongs to you. The power of love hopes all things, believes all things, and endures all things. This unity of love does not rescind itself when we avoid it or pretend that it doesn't exist. Love is an action, not a feeling. Love is what we do for others, which is why it is always available. We just have to put it into action. Sadly, most people wait for the other person to initiate gestures of love, and they end up waiting forever.

Foreplay

It's harder for women to choose to show love and engage intimately when we hurt because women are designed differently than men. Women need more than penetration to enjoy intimacy, and a woman must connect emotionally to her partner for her to feel any level of satisfaction. When we are in pain, it is more difficult to switch gears emotionally. Foreplay helps a woman get in the game emotionally so she is able to connect and be all-in. Foreplay is not the five or ten minutes before penetration; it is the ongoing flirtatious play between two lovers. It is the frequent and daily touches, gazes, kisses, and deep conversations that keep her embers burning and ignite the fires of intimacy. Couples who don't touch, talk, kiss, or caress each other in sensual ways outside the bedroom have difficulty connecting in the bedroom. It is little wonder why they don't feel butterflies anymore—their love is not in action.

Communication

Women who live with chronic pain or fatigue have more issues in the bedroom than others. A lack of communication and unwillingness to talk openly about what is not working or what you need in the bedroom, due to embarrassment or shame, is where challenges in the bedroom start. When women feel unseen, unheard, and unloved, they disconnect from their partner rather than tell them what's wrong. When a woman suffering in pain goes inside herself and shuts down, she stops expressing love and avoids receiving it, focusing more on pain and blocking out pleasure and love. A man may mistake this behavior as moodiness and avoid her rather than asking how he can make his woman feel seen, heard, and loved. Without communication, this is how two lovers become roommates. Tell your partner what is happening and look for solutions together. You are not alone; you are a team.

Intimacy and Sex Relieves Pain

Sex is one of the best remedies to alleviate pain, decrease stress, and rebalance the autonomic nervous system. Yet touch is the one thing that women suffering physically or emotionally pull away from the most. The damage that results from pulling away and isolating from our spouse is quite profound. Our partners can feel unwanted, unneeded, unattractive, and unloved. Because of that, they can also plummet into emotional and physical issues of their own.

Touch is the one thing that women suffering physically or emotionally pull away from the most.

When physical pain is involved, it's not usually for the lack of wanting to be intimate; it's generally because the pain is so debilitating that sexual encounters are no longer fun or enjoyable. Communication from both partners is crucial to find a way to engage with each other in a way that brings pleasure without pain, because a lack of intimacy exacerbates emotional pain and further strains the relationship.

A lack of emotional and physical connection robs and steals relationships. It is destructive, insidious, and devastating. Sexual intimacy and connection alleviate both physical and emotional pain.

Limiting Beliefs

Chronic disease can exacerbate limiting beliefs regarding sexual intimacy and even create faulty beliefs. Due to physical challenges and limitations of disease, many limiting beliefs revolve around our appearance. I had the most ridiculous beliefs along my journey to wellness. At one point I had to wear the most gawdawful sandals in order to walk. I would get dressed up to go out to an event with my Mr. Wonderful and feel hideous because of my shoes. I felt unattractive and very unsexy. I thought Scott would not feel attracted to me because I looked ugly in those shoes. My shoes had nothing to do with how attractive I was to him. What makes us attractive is our heart, our soul, and our zest for life, not the shoes we wear. Although I couldn't wear the stilettos, I changed the story I was telling myself about the shoes and wore them in my heart instead and rocked out those ugly shoes with my passion for life itself.

After learning about the history of women and intimacy, it became painfully clear that I had been lied to about sex, and I had accepted these lies as truths, using them to create my beliefs and rules about what "good sex" was and what it was not. The time had come for me to change my perspective about intimacy and the rules I had created around sex so that my Mr. Wonderful and I could passionately express our love for each other in ways that served and fulfilled us both. When intimacy isn't all about you but rather, how you show up for and please your lover, it makes lovemaking so much better. If you haven't been intimate with your lover due to chronic disease or emotional disconnection, stop using it as an excuse and start exploring pleasure together.

Historically, many men show up for a sexual encounter for themselves. They don't know how to please their woman, or what they have tried hasn't worked, so they give up entirely and just do their own thing. Men are not taught how to pleasure a woman, and women usually don't tell their man what they like or how they want to be touched, either because they don't know themselves or are too shy to say anything.

Couples must learn to communicate with each other, in and out of the bedroom. If you want to experience a loving, intimate, passionate marriage, ladies, you need to tell your man exactly what you like and teach him how to pleasure you. Men are not mind readers, and women are not aroused the same ways as a man, so men need to be taught how to pleasure you. Every pussy is as unique as the woman it belongs to. When a man pleasures and satisfies his woman, she will give it back a hundredfold, and their relationship will soar to greater heights.

My Mr. Wonderful has always known how to give me immense pleasure and sexual fulfillment. I am so thankful that he never gave up on me. He was always adventurous. It was me who was closed off and limiting my own experience because of some ridiculous beliefs and rules about what sex was supposed to be like.

In my darkest moments, riddled with pain, stress, and defeat, he always loved me and tried to pleasure me. He has always known that shifting my focus back to pleasure through touch, intimacy, and holding me tight, even when I didn't want to, would make all the difference.

We can live life barely breathing or we can take in a deep breath of life and use it to awaken the love, passion, and desire we already have within.

Allowing myself to get in the game emotionally, despite pain, fatigue, or feeling unloved, and allow his love to take over my body, mind, and spirit gives me the ability to tap into my creative passion center, release endorphins, and express myself fully, annihilating pain and tapping deeper into pleasure. Because of this deep connection to my lover and myself, I am no longer a prisoner of anger and pain. I am a beautiful, sensual, passionate woman full of love, vibrancy, and joy.

Life is worth living. We can live life barely breathing or we can take in a deep breath of life and use it to awaken the love, passion, and desire we already have within, unleashing it for all the world to experience the rapturous radiance of a woman filled with pleasure.

Do not run away and hide from intimacy. Communicate. Find a way to pleasure your lover and allow your lover to pleasure you. Embarrassment and shame do not feel as fantastic as a mind-blowing orgasm—I guarantee it. Get out of your own way. Tell your lover what you like, and if you don't know, go on an adventure together. Allow passion to reignite you and bring you back to life, regardless of the diagnosis.

Lightbulb Moments to Build Audacity

1. We must pop the bubble on our limiting beliefs to rediscover pleasure.

2. It is vitally important for a woman to embrace her femininity and understand what gives her pleasure mentally, emotionally, and physically, both sexually and nonsexually.

3. To experience pleasure of any type, a woman needs to connect emotionally.

Audacious Actions to Live Well on Purpose

1. Write a love letter to yourself. Tell yourself everything that you love and appreciate about you. Journal three things what you will do to experience pleasure this week.

2. Write a love letter to your lover. Tell them how much you love them. Reflect on some of the things you used to do together in your courtship or early days of marriage that brought you pleasure and intimacy. Let them know what you enjoy sexually and how they can pleasure you even

more. Tell them how you want to please them and what you will do to make that happen.

3. Plan a sensual night of romance. Be creative. Refuse to take a rain check. Hint: do not talk about work, kids, dogs, or anything that does not fuel sensual passion. If you are single, you can plan a romantic evening for yourself. Perhaps that is a candlelight dinner, a sensual bubble bath, and a good movie with decadent chocolate and wine.

CHAPTER 13

She Radiates! Audacity and the Power of Beauty

BEAUTY IS in the eye of the beholder, but have we truly beheld ourselves?

Audacity Is Beautiful

Audacity is the love, strength, and courage to stand up for who you really are, to stand in the face of adversity, pain, emotional torment, and to still radiate love to those around you. When we are who we were created to be, and we live out of the realm of possibility instead of fear, we are a force to be reckoned with, and our beauty is unleashed.

Audacity wasn't something I strived for; I was born with it. God created me to be bold so that I can fiercely show up for myself, my family, and for women who have forgotten who they are or where they are going—to inspire them to rise up, hold their heads high, tap into pleasure, dream their biggest dreams, and never give up until they create the life they've always wanted.

Some women are born with the power of audacity already within them. They have it sewn into every fiber of their being. God gave them this gift to withstand, press in, and get up every single time they fall. As the wind and the waves of life blow and billow, sometimes these women might take a little bit longer to get up, sometimes they get beaten around, and sometimes the wind takes their breath away and knocks them down. But at some point, audacious women remember who they are and where they are going. They rise up and use the same wave that caused them to come crashing down as fuel to propel themselves forward. Audacity causes them to get up and ride on top of that wave, soaring above the hurt and the pain, to find the path forward regardless of the situation or diagnosis.

For some women, audacity can be learned. Maybe they weren't born with a natural boldness to stand up for themselves or their dreams, but they have seen bold women whom they respect successfully achieve their dreams, making them want to pursue their dreams too. They want to be able to undauntedly stare life in the eye, lock in their target, grab life by the horns, and run hard to the finish line. With coaching and practice, we can become audacious and release ourselves from the pain that we have experienced, throwing away our limiting beliefs and changing our inner dialogue so that we can think better, see better, and hear better to reach our dreams.

For other women, audacity must be sought because they have a tendency to hide in the background, letting life happen to them, not realizing they can empower themselves through bold mindsets and actions. Sometimes a diagnosis nails a death sentence to their back and a lightbulb turns on. They realize that they are in the throes of death itself, which cause them to stand up, grit their teeth, and do whatever it takes to regain their life and their health with fierce audacity. For others, the same diagnosis causes them to freeze in fear, retreat, and hide from life, completely letting go of their dreams and life.

Regardless of which type of woman you are, audacity is a muscle that must be trained. We must constantly choose to have the boldness to live well with passion. Connecting with our pleasure and inner beauty allows us to hold our heads high, straighten our crowns, and laugh in the face of adversity. We were made to shine.

I don't get it 100 percent right all the time. I've had twenty-two years of trials that helped train my audacity to rise up faster and faster with every cut, bruise, and fall. I refuse to be crushed, abandoned, or destroyed. I am the audacious wellness warrior. I will rise and fight for my life with every breath, and I will show you how to fight for yours, calling out the boldness and beauty that is within you so that you, too, can be healed and set free.

Tomorrow is too late to start your healing journey. Decide today to have the audacity to fight for your life by taking bold action. We can't just hope that our body will heal on its own. We

We must take charge and command our body back to life and do whatever it takes to live our life, not our diagnosis.

must take charge and command our body back to life and do whatever it takes to live our life, not our diagnosis. It's time to wear your audacity, stand in front of the mirror in your best Wonder Woman pose, look yourself in the eye, and promise to live well every day, no matter what.

Beauty Is Not Skin-Deep

When your body is disfigured due to a disease or an accident, it can be challenging to look at yourself in the mirror and see beauty staring back at you. It can be emotionally difficult to believe that you are beautiful when all you see are the war wounds of life ravishing your body. This is where audacious thinking is crucial. It can help you release your beauty from within regardless of your outer appearance. When you have the boldness to choose to see and accept yourself for who you are inside, your power is unleashed and the disease, deformities, and wounds will no longer have any limits or conditions on your life.

To this day, my Mr. Wonderful tells me I am beautiful. For years I had difficulty accepting this truth. Like many women, I had been brainwashed by magazines, movies, and friends to believe that beauty was skin-deep. I believed that if you did not have a drop-dead gorgeous body, then you needed to cover it, drape it, dye it, pluck it, style it, or dress it to fit in or be seen as beautiful.

Beauty is a state of being. It is who you are deep down at the level of your soul.

The reality is that those ideas are a bunch of man-made marketing schemes designed to deflate, judge, and condemn women into being slaves to the cosmetic and beauty industries at the cost of their self-esteem, mental wellness, and, in many cases, their health. Beauty comes from within. It is not something you can glue on, paint on, change into, perm, color, tattoo, or surgically alter. You cannot command beauty, fake beauty, steal beauty, or erase beauty.

Beauty is a state of being. It is who you are deep down at the level of your soul. Don't allow the deformity of your physical body to dictate the beauty of your soul.

Beauty Is the Radiant Expression of a Loved Soul

When you allow your heart to sing, your soul to soar, and your spirit to fly, there is a radiance, an inner beauty, that emanates from your very essence, and you begin to partner with life on an entirely different level. This acceptance and love of yourself frees you to come alive and radiate with confidence, self-control, loving-kindness, compassion, love, and gentleness toward your-self and those around you. This radiance is your true beauty that's being expressed for the world to see. A woman who walks in power of her inner beauty is extremely attractive because she is fully alive.

When our souls are caught up in negativity and hatred of our own bodies, we become disconnected from our inner beauty and rob ourselves of the power to create and experience pleasure. When you are having a pity party, have you ever noticed that the longer it goes on, the easier it is to stay in that woe-is-me state than to put on your big girl panties and march right out of that life-sucking mood into one of joy, laughter, hope, and love? When we go into dark mode, our souls become negative and lackluster, and we unknow-ingly start plotting a course away from pleasure and toward increased pain. When we avoid tapping into our inner beauty, we not only miss out on life, but other people miss out on experiencing the real you. It is much more pleasurable to be audaciously alive, staring life in the face with hope, than it is to cover our heads with a blanket of negativity and wish life would pass us by.

Pleasure Is Not Just an Emotion; It's a Compass

Many women are driven by their emotions, feeling their way through life based on past experiences and feelings. When women struggle with physical or emotional challenges, they tend to disconnect from pleasure rather than focus on it to help them shift into a more positive state in the moment.

Pleasure is not just a feeling; it is a compass that directs our life.

Being disconnected from pleasure can cause us to emotionally misinterpret the situation, which often directs us toward pain rather than pleasure. Pleasure is not just a feeling; it is a compass that directs our life. Is your compass set toward pain or pleasure? We can discover the direction of our compass based on the emotions that rule our lives.

Emotions can be summed up into two large categories: those that are pleasurable and those that are painful. Just because we experience an emotion doesn't mean we need to coddle it and allow it to fester. For example, when we feel ugly, we can either allow that feeling to consume us and bring us down, or we can be audacious and tap into our pleasure center and ask ourselves what would make us feel more beautiful in this moment—and then go and do it. Whether it is putting on a sexy lipstick, exercising, doing your hair, changing your outfit, or taking a bubble bath, the only requirement is that it brings you back to feeling pleasure, by empowering you to thrive.

The ways we interpret and respond to our feelings can direct our days positively or negatively. No one can make you feel anything. You decide how you feel. Whether you choose to radiate and shine in your awesomeness or whether you choose to carry a rain cloud over your head, you are the only person who can flip the switch on your mood.

When we show up for the day anticipating pleasure, our day is better in every way. We can choose to live our lives discouraged, or we can choose to live with hope and joy despite the challenges. Not to negate the challenges of life—chronic pain, fatigue, and depression are huge trials—but in a state of audacious pleasure, we can live beyond our challenges in anticipation of a beautiful day and a life well lived.

When we show up for the day anticipating pleasure, our day is better in every way.

Society has programmed us to have a reason to show up as less than who we really are, to wallow in self-pity and discouragement, and to downplay our joy and our beauty to avoid offending those around us. We don't need to partner with unhappiness or wear it on our sleeves. We can train our soul to see better, hear better, and think better, lifting ourselves up so we can live beyond our physical appearance, audaciously showing up as the best version of ourselves regardless of what is going on in our body, mind, or relationships. Don't live a single day as anything less than your awesome self.

Stop exaggerating and drowning in negative, life-sucking emotions while "soft-serving" the best parts of your day. It's okay to have a fantastic day despite the pain and hurt. We can't help ourselves or others by hiding from the world. Be a lighthouse. Shining your light empowers other women to turn on their own lights so they can stand audaciously in their own truth and beauty.

We can allow life to intensify our light or to put it out. The choices we make move our compass. I had the audacity to choose life, no matter what. I chose to turn my compass toward healing, not palliation, because I wanted something more for my life than being confined to a wheelchair. This bold action was uncharted territory; there was no map with directions to get myself back to health. At every road bump and detour, I made a conscious choice to turn away from pain and back toward pleasure so that I could live fully. I refused to give up, no matter how difficult the journey was.

I can tell you all the stories of my journey and why I made the choices that I made along the way, but every woman must choose the best path for herself, the path that will allow her to shine the brightest and refuel and recharge her passions, desires, and life itself.

My journey is not about "I am woman, hear me roar." It is about discovering, recovering, and being the beautiful, radiant woman that I am, regardless of my past or the defor-mities of my body. It is about helping women chart a course toward pleasure and healing so they can stand in their own power and claim their beauty, regardless of their diagnosis or outward appearance. When women stop competing with one another and start standing up for, supporting, and encouraging one another by reminding each woman of her unique awesome-ness and beauty, we release healing and give each other permis-sion to live as our most authentic selves. Our beauty is our power because beauty is the true expression of our soul. Being you is powerfully beautiful. There is no one else like you. Stop believing the lies you have been telling yourself. Your diagnosis does not define you; it is not who you are, and it has nothing to do with the beautiful woman that you are.

You are beautiful. Believe it—because it is true. You have just forgotten along the way, as I once did. Thankfully, I had my Mr. Wonderful to remind me who I was on the inside until I could see it for myself. The diagnosis cannot change who you are unless you allow it to by darkening your soul and refusing to shine. I am beautiful inside and out, because beauty is not skin-deep. When you know this, you will tap into your audacity and power. I am here to call you higher and pull you into your beautiful life.

It's your turn. Right now, you can choose to bust loose from your self-inflicted prison, regardless of the diagnosis, emotional pain, or torment of your soul. Will you take the challenge to rise up and be the woman you were created to be? Will you stand up for your pleasure, your beauty, and your life? Will you throw away any values, beliefs, and stinking thinking that has been holding you back and allow your true, beautiful self to shine?

Whatever you choose, let it be authentically and audaciously you. Let your choices plot a course filled with pleasure that moves you into the beautiful life you have always dreamed of living.

Lightbulb Moments to Build Audacity

1. Beauty is all around us and within us. To see beauty in the world, we must first recognize it in ourselves. Be radiant: allow the true you to be expressed in your smile, your words, and your actions.

2. Take responsibility for your life. Stop letting others make decisions that you should be making for yourself.

3. Audacity is about taking surprisingly bold risks. When it comes to your health and your life, take bold actions that are empowering and lifegiving. Life and death matters are not casual decisions. Allow your warrior to come out, take charge, and guide you to decisions that serve you.

Audacious Actions to Live Well on Purpose

1. What negative emotion dominates your life? What emotion/mood can you choose to express instead that will give you more joy in your day?

2. Choose something that you can do starting today to experience pleasure. Write the word "pleasure" on your bathroom mirror in lipstick so you can remind yourself to seek pleasure daily.

3. What do you need to rediscover about your inner beauty and who you are? Journal your thoughts and take bold actions to release your radiance and truth.

CHAPTER 14

Becoming the Dance: The Power of Letting Go

DANCING WAS a huge part of my life. From as early as I can remember, I danced. Spinning and twirling around in our family's living room, having dance parties with my sisters, doing the Limbo with a broom, and spinning one another until we were dizzy. We often went to dancing functions as a family, dancing the night away. It was so much fun. My dad always wore his cowboy boots dancing so he could slide on the dance floor and spin us around in circles so fast that we had to hold on for dear life. I developed a love for dancing and music of all types.

Music was always playing in our home. At night, I would fall asleep to the lulling sounds of Slim Whitman's "Cattle

Call" from the record player downstairs. Music moved me deep within my soul and made me feel alive. Perhaps my love affair with dance began because of the way music helped me to express my emotions.

Growing up, I took Ukrainian dancing classes because it is a part of my maternal heritage, so learning the dance and culture were important to me. I went on to dance competitively, winning many gold medals. My dance troop even performed at Expo '86. I loved the fast beats, the kicking, the jumping, the yelling, and the twirling of all the girls in synchronicity. I loved watching the boys show off their jumps and kicks, and I relished any chance I got to do lifts. There is a passionate expression of life in Ukrainian dancing. Every dance tells a story about life's trials and blessings, harvesting, and the importance of community. Dance brought out the best in me. It taught me to always be on top of my game and do everything with excellence.

I cried for months after I turned in my dancing boots and retired from dancing. It felt like a piece of who I was disappeared. I hung up my dancing boots because I could no longer keep up with requirements to be a competitive dancer, but dance could never be taken out of me; it was a part of who I was.

After I married Scott and started having children, I sang and danced with my kids, bouncing them around the kitchen and twirling them in the living room. When my Mr. Wonderful would come home, we would kiss, embrace, and then dance. We wound our bodies together and danced in the kitchen every night. Occasionally it was just us, two lovers in a moment of passion, but usually we had a kid or four clinging to our legs or dancing on top of our feet.

Dancing moves me to my very core. It helps me to come alive, feel free, and express myself like nothing else. Dancing helps me tap into my creativity and power. Being fully immersed in the soul of the music is a delight to my senses, both physically and emotionally. I feel music deep in my soul. Every note releases joy, hope, grief, passion, and so much more. As I allow the rhythm and the beat of the bass to move my body and soul toward pleasure, I release the stress and pain of the day. Music allows my heart to sing and my soul to soar, and dance sets my spirit free.

As the ankylosing spondylitis progressed, it infiltrated my body like a plague and dance became more challenging for me. I could not embrace my husband without pain, I could no longer touch my body to his, and anything that required jumping or bouncing was totally out of the question. For many years of my life, I could hardly walk, let alone dance. Any type of unexpected movement or jar to my body, such as my Mr. Wonderful grabbing me unexpectedly or the kids bumping into my leg, would send electric shocks radiating up and down my spine and searing pain in whatever body part had been touched. I desperately wanted to dance, but I could not physically make it happen.

A part of me died when I was no longer able to dance. Watching others dance would engulf me with crushing feelings of sorrow as I mourned what I once had. Dancing became a pain point rather than the joy it once was. As my body became more locked down, my spirit shut down and my radiance dwindled.

Many years ago, I went to a Christian conference where the organizers asked people to come to the front to stand and wait on God, listening for what He wanted to say to each person. That night I was determined I was going to get a word from God, that He was going to speak right into the depths of my soul and tell me exactly what He wanted me to do. I was broken inside. I was suffering with pain, and I felt hideous because of the way I looked and walked. I felt like Frankenstein.

As I stood there with my eyes closed and my arms outstretched, the music played in the background. I waited and waited. I heard nothing. I felt nothing. God was silent. I pressed in harder and asked—even begged—God to speak to me. I became acutely aware that people were going back to their seats, yet I stood there with my eyes closed and my arms outstretched, waiting. I was determined to not move until God spoke to me. I didn't even care whether I made a fool out of myself.

This was not normal behavior for me. As much as I am confident and strong, I don't like to be embarrassed or stick out like a sore thumb. Historically, I would have felt pressured by people returning to their seats, and I would have taken my seat feeling disappointed. This day something was different. I really felt like I needed to wait for God to speak to me. In my mind I said, *Lord, even if the preacher starts speaking, I will stand here until You speak to me.*

It had been a long time since I had gone up to the front.

I stood there, with sweat pouring down my back from the pain of standing up so long, waiting on God. Eventually a young prophetic dancer came up to me. She said, "God wanted me to tell you that you will dance again."

I opened my eyes and looked at her with absolute shock and disbelief, wondering how she could say that to me. *Doesn't she see what I look like? I am a hideous, grotesque monster with a deformed body. What would make her think I ever danced before or that I could ever dance again? I can barely stand here, let alone dance. Why would she say that I will dance again?* This sweet young girl just looked at me with absolute love and said with a smile, "God told me that you are a dancer, and you will dance again." And she danced away.

I went back to my seat and cried for the rest of the service. I could not listen to the sermon. I sat there I wondering how it was possible that I would ever dance again. I knew it had to be a message from God because there is no way any person would say something like that on their own from looking at me. I never let go of the promise from God that I would dance again. I wondered how it would ever come to pass, yet I believed.

As the disease progressed, my body locked itself down like a walled fortress out of self-protection. My muscles and fascia were like cement, inflexible and stiff, as if I had been cast in mortar. I had very limited awareness of the right side of my body. If someone was walking on my right side, I could not tell whether they were two inches from me or four feet from me. I was so disconnected from the right side of my body that I would start to panic if someone was on my right-hand side.

My Mr. Wonderful learned to walk only on my left-hand side, but for others, I would casually move to the other side, embarrassed that it caused so much anxiety for me.

This issue went beyond walking. If my chiropractor wanted me to lie on my right side, I couldn't just roll over. I had to get up, walk around the table, sit down, and then lie on my right side. It was like there was a short circuit in my brain. I would tell myself to roll over to the right, and my brain would say, *I don't understand. I have no idea what you are talking about, you can't do this.* It was bizarre. When I had my left hip replaced, the surgical team asked me to roll over onto my right side, and I could not do it. They tried to help me, but as I rolled across the center of the surgical table, my brain totally freaked out and I panicked, grabbing hold of the nurse because I could not tell where the bed was. It felt as though there was no bed at all and I was falling right off the table.

The physiotherapist called it *sensory motor amnesia,* a disconnect of my brain to the right side of my body due to the immobilization of my hip and spine. She said it was like having a stroke. Because I had not been able to use those muscles, tendons, and ligaments for years, my brain "turned them off." It was as if they no longer existed. I had to reconnect my brain to the right side of my body through exercises and relearn spatial relationships all over again. I have come a long way since my hip replacements, but there are still some lingering challenges with fast or unpredictable right-sided movements. I am a work in progress, and I won't give up until my body is totally restored.

Two summers ago, my Mr. Wonderful and I were looking for something to do to connect and have more fun together. I stumbled across an online dancing school for couples and convinced him to purchase a series of lessons so we could spend our evenings learning a few dance moves to get ready for our daughter's upcoming wedding. I'm not going to lie: I was terrified about dancing again because my body was so rigid and stiff, my range of motion was limited, and I couldn't even bounce without feeling my back muscles pull or having my bladder let itself go. But I felt that my mobility had come a long way with my chiropractic and osteopathic treatments. I had more freedom of movement than I'd had in years, and I had a great support team to get me back into tip-top shape if I did hurt myself. And truthfully, the desire to dance was becoming stronger every day. I needed to figure out a way I could dance again.

Our dance lessons were comical at first. We would watch the instruction video, and with looks of horror on both of our faces we would laugh and say, "I don't think we should do that," and then we would try. As we attempted those moves, fear sometimes overwhelmed me, and my brain would shut down and veto my dance move, saying, *Nope, that is not going to happen.* I would freeze in place and say to Scott, "I can't do it. It's too dangerous."

And in his loving and gentle way, my Mr. Wonderful would say, "I bet you can. Let's try it slowly." We would break it down, try, freeze, and try again, and then it would happen! I discovered that I could do those moves. They didn't always look good, and it felt awkward and strange to move my body that way again. It was hard for me to determine where I was in the room in relation to my husband, but we did it. Sometimes I was so nervous about a new dance move that I would start laughing hysterically mid-dance and pee my pants. But we were having fun and doing things I never dreamed would be possible again. My Mr. Wonderful was lifting me into the air, and I was jumping into his arms. He was sliding me along the floor, and it was spectacular. I had to keep reminding myself that I was dancing. It was mentally challenging for me because I kept comparing myself to what my body used to be capable of. What I was feeling and experiencing sometimes left me feeling defeated, like I was letting us down and that I was a lesser version of myself. This was a lie from the pit of hell that was trying to steal my joy of dancing again. I had to constantly pull out my audacious mindset to squash those negative thoughts and keep trying.

Expectation Leads to Disappointment

Seeing my disappointment in myself, my Mr. Wonderful kept encouraging me. "Babe, you're doing it! You are dancing; just be happy with that. It doesn't matter what it looks like. You are dancing!" He would smile, grab me in his arms, and kiss me. My husband is my greatest cheerleader. For that I am eternally grateful. It was challenging not to let negative feelings creep in or to judge myself on what I was doing, what it should look like, or how I could have done it years ago. I had to keep standing on my value, my worth, and my grit to keep trying, no matter what. Shoulds and coulds have no place in an audacious warrior's mind. It didn't matter what it looked like or felt like. I was dancing, and that was all that mattered.

I often hype things up in my mind and am later disappointed because it is not how I had planned it in my imagination. I have learned that if I go into a situation in a peak state, showing up as my best self physically, mentally, and emotionally, this is when the awesomeness happens. This is when my audacious warrior comes out to shine, which increases my experience exponentially, taking it to higher highs.

Even knowing that, I kept wondering when my brain would reconnect with my body and feel that it was safe to just let go, feel the music, and allow the rhythm and the beat to overwhelm my soul. When would I be free to just flow with the music and not worry about hurting myself?

One day we were practicing a spin that I was finding particularly challenging. The spin had me turning over my right shoulder, in a way that I was totally blind to where my husband was. I had to trust him to spin me correctly so I didn't fall into him or torque my back, leaving me injured. It made me so nervous that my brain panicked every time we attempted it, and I would freeze.

Because of the loss of spatial awareness on my right side a few years previously, I didn't comprehend that spin; it was like a foreign language. Scott kept drilling the spin, trying to make it fun for me. It wasn't fun at all—it was outright scary. I had visions of throwing out my back and ending up at the chiropractor every day for the next month. Yet something inside me willed me to keep trying. I pushed my body hard, and I pushed my mind harder.

> *I pushed my body hard, and I pushed my mind harder.*

I started visualizing the dance moves even when we were not dancing, perfecting the moves in my mind. I would try and feel how each component of the dance move felt so that I could override the fear and show my mind that I would be okay. While making dinner, I would practice turning and spinning over my right shoulder to try and normalize the movement for my brain. I would not give up. I would not let fear destroy the possibility of awesomeness. I was convinced there must be a way to get rid of this overactive self-protection mode I had developed. I told myself my Mr. Wonderful would never let me get hurt. I needed to just let go.

I had been trying to lead rather than let my husband do so, partly because I was a dancer and he was not. He didn't really know how to lead, so I was just helping us by leading for him—at least, that is what I kept telling myself. Truthfully, I was leading because I was trying to be in control so I wouldn't get hurt. The problem with that thinking is, when your spouse thinks they are leading and you are not really following them, this is where accidents can happen. It's totally okay to let others lead. Sometimes in life we must follow in order to allow rhythm and flow to enter our lives. I didn't always have to be in control. I could just let go and be free. I had spent most of my life trying to control every situation and circumstance out of fear of being attacked or hurt in some way.

Fear did one thing: it brought me immense pain mentally, emotionally, and physically. Fear pushed me into a life of rigidity, isolation, and pain. Rigidity locked down my body in every possible way and caused me to express only two emotions—rage and grief. I spent years holding myself together, closed emotionally, until the wrong button was pushed. Then I erupted in absolute rage or in a sea of inconsolable tears. I was exhausted from living this way. My emotional responses had since improved substantially, and I was no longer triggered as easily. I was more able to let things roll off my back, and I knew that there was more and that I deserved to be free in my body, mind, and emotions. I did not have to overthink and overanalyze everything that was happening or could happen because of the fear of pain.

Pain is a warning sign that something has gone wrong in the body, but for those with chronic pain, the pain response can also be totally messed up. What we focus on is amplified. In women with chronic pain, the pain receptors are on high alert all the time, making us more aware of anything that could threaten us. Sometimes we even shut down or have an increased pain response when there is a perceived threat so we can avoid the situation all together. This is what was happening to me as I was trying to learn those dance moves. My brain was having a huge emotional response to a perceived threat of possible injury and was trying to keep me safe.

But that night, something rose up in me and in one moment I decided to just let go. The music was playing, and I could feel the beat enter my soul. I felt that I could trust my husband to lead me. I felt total peace, and in that moment, I became the dance.

I became the dance. The music enveloped me. My heart began to sing, and my spirit soared. The steps became easy, rhythmical, and flowing. In that moment the word that young girl spoke over me came true. God said I would dance again, and here I was, dancing in the arms of my Mr. Wonderful. It felt so freaking good. For the first time in many years, I was free. Free from the bondage, free from the pain, free from the torment of my own body. I was the dance, and the dance was me.

Everything shifted in that moment. I felt it; my husband felt it. What started as a fun date night became pure bliss. A part of me that was lost was restored. My heart was singing, and my spirit was soaring. I was alive, and it felt wildly audacious.

Lightbulb Moments to Build Audacity

1. Sometimes we feel that our body needs to be pushed harder when in reality it is our mindset that needs to be pushed beyond the negative thinking and blockages we have put up to self-protect. Kick limiting beliefs to the curb. They do not serve you; they limit you.

2. When you feel like you can't, you must. This is the only way to overcome fear and limiting beliefs. Do it afraid. *Can't* is not in the vocabulary of an audacious wellness warrior.

3. Freedom is not overrated. Strive to set yourself free. Refuse to hold yourself in bondage any longer. Bust out of the prison cell you have built around yourself and live your life well.

Audacious Actions to Live Well on Purpose

1. What has fear cost you? What has changed because of fear? Write a list so you can see how fear has sidelined you, then make a new list of what you will no longer allow fear to control in your life. Read this list daily to remind yourself to stand in your power and truth.

2. What part of your life do you need to let go a bit more to experience freedom? Choose one area you would like to feel more alive, and commit to pressing into freedom in this area. Journal your action plan in your favorite pen color to remind yourself of how audacious you are.

3. Decide to try something you haven't done in a long time that you used to love. Schedule it on your calendar and have a close friend hold you accountable to do it. Enjoy every moment.

PART 3

Steps Forward

CHAPTER 15

No Time for Pain: The Power of Mindset

PAIN CAN BE fleeting and complex, affecting us both physically and emotionally. Pain exists entirely outside of the physical body and can be perceived emotionally from a distance or memory. Pain is felt in our brain and stored in our memories and has deep emotional connections. Pain is complicated.

What is really going on behind and beyond the sensations of discomfort, affliction, and downright agony? Why does one person seem to have more pain than another? What causes an increase in pain perception? What mindset allows one person to flourish when they are being tormented by pain and another to lock down, pull the covers over their head, and lie in bed for days or weeks? It comes down to our own unique perception of pain.

Everyone has pain receptors, but they are triggered differently in each person and are based on historical events and the language and meaning we gave to the situations that caused us pain in the past. The meaning we give to an event links the sensation of pain to an emotion. People perceive pain differently because of their own emotional perceptions. There is much to say about the psychology and impact on a child from a helicopter parent who overreacts to every bump or knock versus the parent who smiles and reassures the child with a hug and a kiss that they are okay. One child grows up acutely aware of every potential injury and has a heightened response to pain, while the other may shrug off pain even when it is serious.

The perception of and response to pain can completely shift in a moment based on our focus; hormones, such as endorphins; and the situation or environment itself. Let's consider childbirth. One of the reasons why Lamaze breathing is so effective during labor is because it helps the mother focus on her breathing rather than the pain. Deep breathing causes the heart rate and breathing to slow down and sync up, causing the brain to release endorphins to help calm the mama and decrease her perception of pain. When the baby is born, the pain suddenly decreases as a cascade of hormones floods the body: oxytocin (the love or cuddle hormone), beta-endorphins (the hormones of pleasure and transcendence), epinephrine and norepinephrine (the hormones of excitement), and prolactin (the mothering hormone). Within seconds, the worst pain of your life vanishes as you gaze lovingly into the eyes of your newborn baby. These hormones help women write the story of labor with a pleasurable and rewarding ending; otherwise, we would never want to have another child.

For women who've had multiple babies, the moment we feel that first true contraction with subsequent labors, our memory banks fire up and, like a deer in the headlights, we suddenly remember the pain that is about to let loose in our body. As every bit of pain comes flooding back into our minds, we remember the pleasurable ending to the story of labor and immediately shift our focus, take a few deep breaths, and decide to take it one contraction at a time because we know the story and we know that the reward for labor is spectacularly wonderful.

Our mindset is crucial in every aspect of our life, whether it's living day to day, having a baby, or seeking how to live free from pain and suffering.

Focusing on Pain Increases Pain

When we choose to focus on pain, that is exactly what we will experience: pain and more pain, until we fall asleep exhausted. If you go searching for pain, you can always find it.

It's fascinating how we can go through our day laughing

If you go searching for pain, you can always find it.

and having fun enjoying the company of a friend and have very little pain, but when we go back home to real life, all the pain comes back with a vengeance. We may be visiting friends, having a great time, and not really feeling any pain because we are relaxed and focused on something other than ourselves.

Pain intensifies when we are not living life fully alive. When we are stressed, hungry, anxious, angry, or sleep-deprived, we don't cope as well, and our nervous system becomes more irritated, exponentially increasing our perception of pain. We may even say things such as, "I can't handle this pain." We are more aware of pain when we are tired, grumpy, or irritated, and our perception of pain increases the more down we feel. When

Every moment of every day has the potential to be awesome and amazing if we let it.

we are not living our best life physically or emotionally, our focus narrows to ourselves, and we move away from pleasure, which highlights pain.

We can ignore pain, coddle it, increase it exponentially, and remove it entirely simply by our thoughts because we are in control of our mindset. Every moment of every day has the potential to be awesome and amazing if we let it. We get to choose what we focus on. We can choose to have fun, love life, and let the little things roll off our backs, or we can choose to be angry, grumpy, sad, lonely, depressed, and miserable. Our mindset affects every area of our life, including how we perceive pain. A miserable mindset contributes to chronic pain.

Pain Robs Our Memories

More than an injury, anxiety, fear, and anger can exponentially magnify pain. In my thirties, I was consumed by anxiety and fear. The pain I experienced every moment of every day was 100 out of 10, without exaggeration. I have no idea how I survived those years. I was engulfed by pain. There are seven years of my children's lives for which I was physically present, but I was mentally and emotionally checked out as I lived as a shadow of myself. The only thoughts I had were of fear, pain, and self-protection. It is extremely upsetting for me to admit that I have very few memories of my children when they were growing up. I was there, I went through the motions, but I was so walled in and armored from pain that I did not actually participate on any meaningful level. My Mr. Wonderful knows the look I get in my eyes when my kids are talking about a fond memory from their childhood and the sad emptiness comes across my face when the memory does not register in my mind. No matter how hard he tries to describe the memory to me, I can't find it anywhere. A life of pain is brutal, not just for the person experiencing the pain but for the entire family as well. For many, pain is a hope killer, a fun stealer, and a relationship destroyer.

Pain Is a Thief: It Steals, Kills, and Destroys

A key component to busting free and overcoming pain is understanding how our mind and body are connected.

The kids were young and my daughters had been asked to clean their room. Rather than cleaning their room, they were fooling around, throwing things, and making forts on their bunk beds, basically making a bigger mess. My patience was low and I had already gone in numerous times to get them back on task. After hearing some loud noises followed by crying, I went to the room with the last straw of my patience being drawn and started yelling at my kids about what they were doing and asking why they were not cleaning their room. My girls were giggling and clearly not listening to me. My anger increased, and so did my voice. I could feel the pain in my back intensifying, and I became acutely aware that the more I yelled, the worse the pain got. Suddenly I realized that my anger was increasing the pain. Dumbfounded, I quickly lowered my voice to a whisper, told the girls to just clean their room, and walked down the hall.

Are You serious? I spoke to God under my breath. *This pain is all because I'm angry? You've got to be kidding me! Lord, why did You not show me this before? I can't believe this is all about anger. Father, I am so sorry. Help me get rid of this anger. I am not an angry person; that was me yesterday. That is totally not me today. Today I have been washed clean by the blood of Jesus. The old angry me is dead, and the new loving, grateful me is alive. Help me Jesus,* I cried. And in that moment, just as quickly as I had noticed the pain increasing, the pain left.

Our emotions connect profoundly to our sense of pain. We've all had the experience of injuring ourselves at home when we are having a bad day versus injuring ourselves at a public event. The same injury feels a whole lot less painful when we're out having fun, and we respond more calmly. Our minds are phenomenally impressive. We have no limits. Our bodies will do anything we tell them to do. There are countless stories of people being told they would never walk, talk, or move again—until they proved their doctors wrong. Deciding what you want to do and doing it despite the limits of your mind or diagnosis is the audacious mindset. Remember, my surgeon told me it was physically impossible for me to walk into his office, except I didn't know that, so I walked anyway.

When you are free from the pain of the past and the limiting beliefs you have created around your traumatic history, you can convince yourself to do anything. Where there is will, there is always a way. If you can't go through it, go under it, go around it, go above it, go beneath it, go beside it—just go. The only limitation is the limit set by your mind. Refuse to shut down, lock down, or crawl into a hole of deception, despair, and pain. Overwrite the programming that puts up limits and barriers. Choose to reframe and see your life from a better perspective.

Pain Is Isolating

Whether our pain is physical, emotional, or spiritual, it siphons the life right out of us. Pain is isolating, destructive, and self-sabotaging. Pain causes us to shrink away and withdraw from engaging with those around us, contracting and sheltering in place in the comfort of our own beds, away from people, noise, fun, laughter, and life itself. Pain causes an isolation that is unlike any other.

Pain causes most women to retreat internally, pulling away from the world to go deeper inside themselves to escape the suffering. Yet when we do this, it causes isolation and immeasurably more pain to ourselves and our relationships. The more pain we are in, the more we pull away from those we love, even though this is when we need their support the most. Isolation causes us to resort to our own dark, depressing thoughts that only reinforce the story we are telling ourselves about why life is horrible. When the only thoughts that cross your mind are some version of "woe is me," it's hard to snap out of it on your own. Isolation enhances our pain whereas relationships bring us comfort.

Living with Pain

Pain is insidious. It may start as a small discomfort, but if left unmastered it can grow and become consuming, destroying every aspect of our lives. The question is not how I can live *in* pain but rather, how I can live *with* pain. It comes back to mindset, the way I choose to think about it, feel about it, talk about it, and react to it. Mindset changes everything.

Reframing is a spectacular tool I have used for years to shift my focus. The language I use to describe a situation and the meaning I give to it can rewrite the story of the situation in a way that gives me pleasure or serves me rather than seeing it in a way that limits me or causes pain.

The more pain we are in, whether it is emotional or physical, the more we stop living and experiencing our life and the more sedentary, less involved, and lonelier we become. Loneliness adds a second dimension to pain, falsely communicating to our mind that we are unlovable and that nobody wants to be around us. The reality is that we choose to pull away from people in an attempt to self-protect; others do not pull away from us. Walling ourselves off from loved ones does not protect us from anything other than enjoying life.

When my kids were young, the pain due to the ankylosing spondylitis was at its peak. A friend would often invite me and the kids over on a hot summer day to spend the afternoon in their swimming pool. *That's a great idea*, I would think to myself. *Too bad I am too exhausted, too tired, and in too much pain to take my kids anywhere.* I knew we would really enjoy the swim and the visit, but it was overwhelming to even think of going, so we usually stayed home. With the pain and fatigue that I had, the thought of packing up four kids under the age of eight, walking a block in the scorching heat, and having to be in the pool to supervise my kids so they didn't drown was like asking me to run a marathon blindfolded, with my arms tied behind my back. I had no energy, no patience, and was not interested in having any fun. Or at least that is what I told myself. It was not true. I desperately wanted to have fun. I just didn't know *how* it was possible to have fun and enjoy life when I was in so much pain and exhausted to the point that I could hardly function.

I lost friends over this. They didn't understand why I couldn't just come over. I had a hard time sharing what it was like to live in my body. I wanted to pretend I was normal and didn't want people knowing how bad it really was. In hindsight, being more open with my friends and family could have alleviated a lot of stress and expectation for all of us. Perhaps we could have found ways for us to get together that were easier on me and less stressful for them.

Socializing with friends helps us shift our focus and momentarily forget about the pain. Friends also laugh together. Laughter is wonderful medicine. Laughter releases endorphins, the *exact* same hormones that give you a runner's high or feelings of elation after an orgasm. Endorphins block the perception of pain in the body and make us feel good. Sadly, people living with chronic pain don't tend to laugh a lot because the pain tends to squelch their zest for life.

One day after school my son, who was twelve at the time, was telling a story about something funny that had happened at school. Everyone was listening intently to his story, and when he got to the funny part, it was so hilarious that everybody started laughing, including me. I laughed so hard that I was doubled over with tears running down my cheeks, and I couldn't catch my breath. Everyone stopped laughing and stared at me. All my kids were looking at me as though it were the strangest thing they had ever seen. It was my son who finally spoke.

"That must have been really funny, because Mom's laughing, and she never laughs." Those words hit me like a ton of bricks. My kids didn't think that I laughed—ever. My son couldn't remember me laughing, and it broke my heart. Who had I become? The chronic pain had affected me deeply. I had turned off emotionally and had disconnected myself for self-protection at the expense of enjoying life to the fullest. I didn't laugh because I didn't feel anything but pain. Life was anything but fun.

I decided I had to change my perspective and redirect my focus. I had four beautiful children, and I refused to miss out on any more of their lives. I wanted to enjoy these kids whom I had yearned for. Do not let pain steal your laughter. We don't have to live in pain but until we can free ourselves from it, we can learn to live well and enjoy life regardless of pain by reframing our situation and the story we are telling ourselves.

Lightbulb Moments to Build Audacity

1. The meaning and language we give to pain shapes and defines how we experience life and how we show up. Show up in a beautiful state every day by choosing to change your focus.

2. Our emotional response has a huge impact on our perception of pain. Reframing with a positive mindset can help reduce pain by bringing more joy to your day.

3. Stay focused on where you are going, not where you have been.

Audacious Actions to Live Well on Purpose

1. Watch a funny movie that you know makes you laugh out loud to release your feel-good happy hormones. Record how you feel before and after the movie. Note the differences in how your body and mind feels and how your outlook on life or today's trials may have changed.

2. Catch yourself in your stinking thinking and reframe your language to change your perception to a more positive one. Yes, you can do this!

3. Next time you feel moody or find yourself fixating on emotional or physical pain, get up, put on your favorite song, and dance out the frustration passionately until all negativity is released. It doesn't matter what it looks like. If you can only move your arms or sway in place, do it. Move your body, allowing all the emotions to move through you until you feel happiness and peace.

CHAPTER 16

I Feel Good! Audacious Strategies to Live Pain-Free

PAIN IS NOT just a physical sensation. It lives outside of your physical body and is experienced in the brain. When a body part is injured, the pain receptors are triggered; they send a signal to the brain, and the brain says, *Ouch! That hurts.* Pain is completely subjective and is totally an individual experience. It is designed for self-protection, a warning system to alert the brain there is a potential issue. When you are too close to a fire, the brain warns you to move back because the temperature is too hot; when you touch a hot stovetop, the brain screams at you to lift your hand because your skin is burning.

Pain can also be emotional. *Don't walk down a dark alley alone late at night. Remember what happened to Sally? Don't shop at that store. Remember when the clerk made fun of you when your credit card was declined and everyone in line started laughing?* Pain sends warning signals and causes us to be more alert and aware. Pain forces us to reconsider our actions instantaneously. Everything we experience has a mental and emotional component. Certain situations can cause physical pain because the brain has associated certain places, events, smells, tastes, and even people with pain. Triggers cause the brain to go back into its own history books, your memories, and find a similar situation and respond based on historical perspective rather than what may be happening in the moment. Since pain is an emergency warning system, anything that the brain associated with pain in the past will cause the brain to perceive pain in the present. This is why one moment you may feel no pain and the next moment you smell something or hear something, or someone says something, and suddenly you feel intense pain.

Reframing helps us respond to pain rather than react to it.

We can retrain how we respond to pain by a technique called *reframing*. Reframing helps us respond to pain rather than react to it. We reframe by choosing to look at a situation in a way that serves us or puts us in a beautiful state rather than steals us of our day or depletes us. The more we reframe historically painful situations in a positive or pleasurable way, the less reactive we will become. For example, we can reframe going to the dentist as a pleasurable experience by listening to our favorite music, asking to watch a movie (they are not just for kids!), or wearing calming essential oils to decrease our stress response and therefore decrease anticipatory pain.

There are other common strategies used to reduce or eliminate pain. The fun of living begins when we realize that we can do many things to help shift our mindset and reduce pain.

Laughter

Laughter is a fantastic way to lighten your mood and reduce pain. Experiencing joy is well known to alleviate pain. Laughter releases endorphins and increases oxygenation. It's a great distraction from our problems and helps us find better solutions faster because our mind becomes more alert due to the increased oxygen and release of our own happy hormones. Laughter is a bonding experience, and that helps us connect deeply with those around us in a relaxing and enjoyable way. Life is too short not to laugh daily. Forget about a little snort; I'm talking about full-on belly laughter that causes tears to run down your cheeks. That kind of laughter helps you reframe your mood and your day. Create your own laughter. You may be amazed at how quickly your pain subsides.

Essential Oils

Essential oils are fragrant organic chemicals found in plants. When we breathe in these aromatic compounds, they have specific, measurable, and repeatable effects on the body's limbic system, which is the seat of our subconscious and where our emotions are formed. Pure, unadulterated essential oils trigger positive emotions in our subconscious and can initiate the release of endorphins, serotonin, dopamine, GABA, and other feel-good hormones. Regular use of aromatic compounds can rewire the brain to respond more positively to various situations that were formerly wired to respond negatively with fear, anxiety, or even pain.

My own journey with essential oils began right after my first hip replacement. At that point in my life, I had chronic fatigue, as most chronic disease sufferers do. I also had severe adrenal fatigue and was very sleep-deprived. Because of this, I was going through a lot of emotional turmoil and mood swings. I was irritated most of the time, and my fuse was short. I went to work, turned myself on for my clients, then crashed afterward.

When we don't sleep, our hormones quickly get out of balance, and so do our emotions and our mood. To clarify, emotions come from our subconscious based on past experiences, and our mood is our response to the emotions. When something happens to us, in a nanosecond our brain searches for a similar memory, one that sounds, looks, feels, tastes, or smells like a comparable experience. Then that emotion rises into our conscious thoughts and we make a choice on how to respond to our emotions, which is our mood.

We can always reframe what we are feeling based on who we are with and the circumstances of what is happening and choose to shift our mood to a more favorable one. Before my hip replacement, my mood was less than stellar. I was not able to reframe or shift out of a negative mood quickly, and I was not rocking out my days. When I first started using essential oils, I used them primarily for emotional and hormonal stability. Within a couple of days of using them, I was sleeping better, my mood was more positive, and my hormones were stabilizing. These gifts of the earth were remarkable. Not only did they smell great but their positive effects on my life were undeniable. I felt like a new woman. I was experiencing happiness, peace, and hope simply by smelling a drop or two of essential oils. Nature has the remarkable power to shift the way we experience life and gives a more positive outlook, which comes right from the level of our very own subsconscious.

Walking through an evergreen forest or an herb garden can have similar effects due to the aromatic compounds naturally found in trees and herbs.

Chocolate

Dark chocolate can alleviate pain and elevate mood. An occasional delectable treat can feed the soul and offer some important nutrition as well. Dark chocolate is full of alkaline minerals such as calcium and magnesium, which can help relax the muscles and ligaments to ease pain and stiffness. Chocolate also releases endorphins and serotonin, your happy sunshine hormone.

Be aware of chocolate that is loaded with sugar. Sugar defeats the purpose of eating chocolate and creates inflammation and pain in the body. It's as simple as making better choices when it comes to eating chocolate. If you think you have a chocolate addiction because you crave a lot of sugar-laden milk chocolate, you don't really have a chocolate addiction: you have a sugar addiction. Call a spade a spade and work your way up to enjoying nutrient-rich 75–85 percent dark chocolate that can benefit your health rather than sabotage it. Go for the good stuff. It may cost more, but the trade-off is worth it: you will eat less, feel better, and be more satisfied.

Exercise

Exercising can be frustrating and onerous for many who are experiencing pain. If you have been sitting or lying around too long, your body seizes up and locks itself in place, just like an old rusty bike chain. Any movement is better than no movement. It sounds contradictory because we often hear that when we have injured ourselves, we should lie down, put our feet up, and do as little as possible to help the injury heal. This advice is for acute injuries such as a sprained ankle or a pulled back from too much gardening.

Rest does not apply to chronic pain in the same way. As part of our built-in self-protection mechanism, chronic pain sufferers naturally try to move as little as possible to limit any pain. The stiffer you are, the more pain you experience because constant immobility contributes to increased stiffness and results in increased pain when you move. When immobilized, the muscles and tissues hold on to lactic acid, a natural by-product of metabolism, creating even more pain. The muscles and supporting tissues then start to contract due to immobility and become increasingly more stiff and sore. Lack of regular movement creates the never-ending vicious cycle of pain, causing you to lock down even more, restricting more movement until your whole body seizes up and something as simple as a sneeze or misstep can send your whole body into spasm and excruciating pain for weeks. Immobility seems like a great idea to limit the pain; however, it causes greater issues, such as decreasing one's mobility, exacerbating pain, and increasing isolation. Move it so you don't lose it.

No One Has Time to Put Their Life on Hold for Pain

Life is too short to put it on hold. You may not get a tomorrow. The fact that you are reading this means you woke up today and discovered you were breathing. Automatically your response

Life is too short to put it on hold.

should be, "Hallelujah! I am alive! It's a great day!" Because the six-feet-under alternative is not a better option.

If you find yourself consumed by pain, change your focus, reevaluate your mood, and get up and move your body. When we move our body, our energy increases and our mood naturally improves. Movement creates change because it forces us to shift our focus. Do a happy dance in your chair, rock out to your favorite song, or go outside and take a walk. Movement is life. It creates flow and increases energy and alertness. Movement releases the body from the prison of negative emotion and pain.

Refuse to live a lesser life of pain and misery. Happiness comes from within, so make your own happiness. Stop relying on others to make or break your day. Choose joy, and do not settle for anything less. I double dare you. No one is promised tomorrow. Don't miss out on today.

Lightbulb Moments to Build Audacity

1. Pain is not felt in the physical body; it is felt in the brain. Learning to reframe your perception of pain is key to overcoming it.

2. Pain is attached to memory through historical events, people, emotions, and smells. Current situations are perceived through the lens of our past. We can rewire our historical perceptions to decrease pain.

3. Every moment of every day has the potential to be awesome and amazing if we allow it to be. When you find your focus shifting toward pain, snap yourself back into focusing on something more positive.

Audacious Actions to Live Well on Purpose

1. Find something that can make you laugh out loud for at least ten minutes a day. Schedule time for your daily laugh.

2. Source some high-quality dark chocolate. Do not settle for just any chocolate. Educate yourself on dark chocolate. Record your tasting experience and note how you felt before and after.

3. Choose a simple way to move your body every day. Make an unbreakable date with yourself to get your body moving to maintain or improve your range of motion and your endurance.

CHAPTER 17

Engage Your Wellness: Empowered Living

MY WHOLE LIFE I have refused to give up. I have always tried to find a way to figure it out and make it work, no matter what, including my healing journey.

Refusing to get in that wheelchair was the best decision I could have ever made. Refusing to accept the projected course of a lesser life because of a diagnosis was almost entirely unheard of. Many people couldn't understand why I was putting myself through such physical and emotional duress rather than just taking the easy way out and getting in that wheelchair. Never in my wildest dreams would I ever have considered a wheelchair to be a choice, let alone an option. I was Wonder Woman; I would find a way. In my mind, the only choice was to live well, and to do that, I needed to get at the root of what was going on in my body and fix it.

The scriptures say, "But let your 'Yes' be 'Yes,' and your 'No,' 'No.'" (Matt. 5:37). I said *yes* to living my life with health and vitality. I said that there was no way in hell I would ever get into that wheelchair, and I meant it. I could not go back on my promise to myself. I would not be wishy-washy with my life.

One of the greatest obstacles to healing is our lack of determination and resolve to stay committed to a wellness lifestyle. We give way too much power to what others think or say about how we should live. In doing so, we allow other people's opinions to cheat, lie, and steal from our life at the expense of our own mental, emotional, physical, and spiritual wellness. Sometimes we even allow the opinions of others to overrule our own values or beliefs in order to avoid conflict. No one else lives your life, walks in your shoes, or lives in your body. Therefore, no one else can make decisions for your life. They just don't have the authority to do so, unless you give it to them by not taking responsibility for your own life. Sometimes it seems easier to allow others to make life-altering decisions for us, but that is always a cop-out. We need to make decisions that serve us, that honor who we are and what we want out of this life. No one has the right to make health decisions for us that can affect our life or the quality of it. However, if someone sees you living a lesser life than what is possible for you, they have every right to encourage and empower you to engage your life, live well, and shine as the radiant woman you are. We are the best keeper of our lives because only we can choose to take the daily actions that are required for us to live well.

No matter how challenging it was to go outside the medical system, to find my way back to wellness and life itself, I made choices that served me and honored my body to live well. Sometimes our choices upset other people even though the choice doesn't affect their life in any way. Going against the status quo can be challenging, but you are not the status quo; you want more for your life.

For example, I eat a starch-free diet to prevent inflammation and pain in my body. My diet challenged my friends because I would not deviate from it regardless of how yummy the food was. Occasionally I went hungry at a party because there was nothing I could safely eat, which stressed them out. Knowing what is best for your body and sticking to it is audaciously loving yourself. I have since learned to always bring a big dish of something I can eat everywhere I go so I can help alleviate social awkwardness and have enough to share.

My refusal to eat grains of any type pushed the envelope for most people I knew. Some of my close friends would get upset when I wouldn't eat the birthday cake, saying that I didn't like their baking. If someone needs me to eat cake to feel valued, there is a much bigger issue driving that thought process. What I eat should not affect your security as a woman, baker, or friend. Compromising our health based on others' reactions can be a huge issue for women who are learning to live an empowered life.

Food Is a Social Influencer

We use food in every type of situation. It is the focal point of our gatherings. We eat when we are happy and when we are sad. We eat at weddings and funerals, at the hockey game, and at the cinema. People generally feel more relaxed when everyone is eating, especially if they are all eating the same thing. Food is a community builder—and a community disruptor. Have you ever noticed that when people decide to start working out and eating better, their friend circle changes? Suddenly they hang out only with health nuts or their friends from Pilates. Perhaps we know that we won't get the support we need from our friends, so we instinctively hang out with people that will encourage us to keep going with our new healthy lifestyle.

Socially it is common to try and convince people who are dieting or trying to make healthy lifestyle changes to cheat on their plan, just this once. Just this once eventually becomes daily, and before they know it, their new healthy lifestyle is nonexistent. Supporting ourselves and our loved ones in their wellness journey is as simple as providing healthier snacks or meals when we gather or not serving their favorite high-calorie food out of consideration for their new lifestyle.

It is crucially important to resolve why we want to get healthy before we start on a restrictive diet, exercise routine, or wellness lifestyle. If we don't know why we are wanting to be healthy, it is easy to fall off the wellness wagon when we are having a bad day or experience a little persuasion from friends.

Next Level Commitment

When we know why we've made a decision to save our life and get our health back, it takes our wellness journey to the next level. This is when audacity will take over and you will stay committed to your wellness plan, no matter what. Someone can offer you your favorite food and you won't even drool, you will leave an amazing party early because you promised yourself to be in bed by 9:30 every night, and you don't drink the champagne at your daughter's wedding because you gave up alcohol to heal your liver. Audacious commitment does not jeopardize health for momentary satisfaction.

Audacious commitment does not jeopardize health for momentary satisfaction.

The greatest challenge after my decision to choose life was not my friends getting upset or my restrictive diet itself; it was the uncharted territory of reversing autoimmune disease and finding practitioners who could partner with me and believed it was possible to regain my health.

I didn't know of anyone who had reversed ankylosing spondylitis. It was arduous to find information about this insidious disease, let alone natural treatment strategies, and the Internet was just becoming a thing when my journey back to life began. Today we live in a world where in a nanosecond you can find information and research articles on any topic you can think of, making it easier than ever to find options to reverse or placate autoimmune disease and live an amazing and abundant life.

Unfortunately, many women do not want to give up anything in order to regain their life. They want to live the same life they have always been living, burning the candle at both ends, stressing out and being anxious, carb-loading, overdosing on coffee or diet soda, and not sleeping. Yet somehow, they believe the pain should stop without them making any changes. It just doesn't work that way. When you keep doing the same things that brought you into your state of suffering and refuse to acknowledge that these lifestyle choices may have caused your health crisis in the first place, there is a limiting belief that is blocking the way to your health freedom. Most women would rather survive on adrenaline, caffeine, and sugar than thrive on sleep, balance, and a healthy metabolism because it is hard for them to make a commitment to themselves and their vitality.

The reason why the medical system says there is no cure for autoimmune disease is because very few people will do what it takes to turn their health around. Genetics aside, we must understand that our lifestyle brought us to the point of a diagnosis and subsequently the shutdown of our body, mind, and emotions. The culmination of stress; a diet of sugar, grains, dairy, and caffeine; a negative mindset; sleep deprivation; worry; guilt; anger; shame; grief; and an inability to detoxify and eliminate the garbage from our bodies and minds set us up to crash and burn or rust and rot away. Genetics are manipulated by our lifestyle; therefore, the bottom line is that our state of health or disease comes down to lifestyle choices.

Healthspan, Not Lifespan

Life is not just about existing; it is about thriving. Without quality of life, longevity is not all it's cracked up to be. It's about healthspan, not lifespan. What good is it to live to be one hundred years old if I spend the last twenty years of my life staring at a wall, unable to communicate or engage with the world around me?

It's about healthspan, not lifespan.

Our bodies are made by God to constantly and continuously recover, repair, heal, restore, and regenerate indefinitely. When we give our bodies the fuel they require to function and perform as the high-performance machines they are, they will serve us well. But if you fill your beautiful Porsche of a body with nutrient-depleted food and empty calories, it might taste good, but eventually your engine will clog and your car will no longer be roadworthy. To have healthspan we need proper fuel in our tanks.

A key and rarely discussed factor in choosing to engage your wellness is mindset. The ability to engage with one's life to the fullest is essential for lifespan and healthspan. It is important to take charge of our life, to take responsibility for who we are and how we show up. We cannot show up as our best, authentic self if we are cowering in a corner afraid to breathe, move, and live. Each of us is born with potential. What we were created to manifest in our lives is something so spectacular and glorious that no other human being ever has or ever will be able to exhibit it to the world. We are that unique and special. However, when we partner with sickness and disease, our potential awesomeness begins to diminish, flicker, and eventually disappear altogether as we turn away from the woman we were made to be.

Many women with chronic disease find themselves living a shadow of their former selves, leaving their hopes and dreams in the past and living from day to day—even moment to moment—just trying to get through the day. Refuse to be the woman who prays to just get through the day. Be the one who runs hard to the very last moment, thrives despite the circumstances, and wins in life by showing up as the beautiful woman she was created to be.

Be Your Own Color

I want women everywhere to show up as the magnificent color they were created to be. Consider a box of crayons. We can get huge boxes of crayons that have multiple shades of the same color. If we look at a color wheel, we can see that there are hundreds of shades of every color, just like women.

If you choose the color pink, what intensity and shade of pink would you pick? If ten ladies sit together in a room with a color wheel, and they all choose pink as their favorite color, undoubtedly every lady would select a different shade of pink. What if on the count of three all the ladies revealed the shade of pink they had chosen? Within a few seconds, the ladies would start comparing other women's color selections to their own and start doubting their choice, even though a few moments before it had been their favorite. Comparison is a stealer of joy. Many of the women will end up liking someone else's shade of pink better. This happens because of our own insecurities about who we are, how we fit into the world, and how we make decisions. We want to be like everyone else, and we want to be liked by everyone else. Not surprisingly, most women will like the shade of pink chosen by the most popular or most influential woman in the room more than the one they selected.

The moral of the story is this: stop trying to be somebody else's shade of pink. Every other color in the crayon box has been taken. You can't be someone else's color. Be the unique color you were created to be. It's time to stand up, take charge, be audacious, and go for it with every fiber of your being. Decide today to choose to engage with your life and run full speed ahead. Decide to not just get your life back but to be the best version of who you were created to be. This is your destiny. This is your time to shine and rise up with audacity on your wings.

Ask Deep Questions

If you are even a wee bit hesitant to live your color, hunt down whatever is holding you back from truly engaging with the beautiful, amazing, radiant, resilient, and audacious woman you were created to be. When we decide to engage with our life, we must go deep into the core of our being, take out the life-sucking trash, and replace it with a beautiful garden of flowers that brings us back to pleasure and life. Refuse to stop at surface level. If you ask yourself a surface-level question, you will get a surface-level answer that will not change or revolutionize any part of your life or well-being.

Dig deep into the core of who you are and ask yourself the soul-searching questions you are afraid to answer because you don't know how you could ever be the woman who could measure up. Stop disqualifying yourself from the goodness of life. The goodness that we desire lives on the other side of our fears and insecurities. The life that we truly desire is hidden by the fear of being ourselves and by a mindset that is hinged on other people's thoughts, feelings, and actions rather than our own.

It's startling to realize that the biggest thing holding us back from living the life we want is our own mind and our limiting beliefs about who we are. We all have belief systems; the problem is, most of our belief systems are total BS. They are nothing but lies and convolutions of the truth. Along the way we have adopted our belief systems based on our interpretation of previous experiences and how people have treated us. These interpretations may or may not be truthful, yet we hold on to them as gospel and they continue to impact us negatively, tainting our view of ourselves and our capabilities, and limiting our ability to achieve the state of health and life we desire.

Limiting beliefs are like roadblocks convincing us that we can't or shouldn't do something—that we are not good enough, smart enough, brave enough, or pretty enough. Empowered living is knowing that *we are enough*. Showing up alive in our radiant enoughness is what will set the world ablaze.

The Heart of a Warrior

Every woman is a warrior at heart. A warrior knows exactly what she wants and exactly how to get it. We have been led to believe that a woman is not powerful or in charge of her own body and mind. We have been told that we don't know what we want or what is good for us, that we need someone else to tell us what is best for our life. Unfortunately, this mindset often leads a woman astray and pushes her further away from her desires and pleasure altogether. No one else knows what you want or what is best for you. We can support one another's dreams and desires, but we each need to have our own dreams and live our own life. Engage with your inner warrior to rediscover the passionate, radiant, powerful woman that you are. The woman who stands up for herself, defends herself, loves lavishly, flirts with life, laughs uncontrollably, and seizes every moment to live out loud and claim the goodness of the day is the audacious woman who will rupture the limiting barriers and expand into her destiny full of life and vitality.

Engage Your Wellness

Engaging your wellness means being morally committed to capturing, seizing, attracting, or captivating your wellness, to be more pointed, to be engrossed and captivated in taking back your health. When we are not operating from our authentic self, we want to hide, step back, reassess, and contemplate rather than act. We want to maintain the status quo no matter how painful or life-sucking it is. Sadly, fitting in with others is more important to many women than their own health and life.

In clinical practice, I've seen countless women who are fed up with suffering through life in pain. They leave their appointment excited about their new wellness plan and the possibility of feeling better, but then they go home to a less than supportive husband and family, who pressure them to make unhealthy meals, to stay up late, and to "just eat the cake." Initially they may have great resolve and refuse to engage with the attempted sabotage of their wellness plan. But as their friends keep pressuring them to do whatever it is "just this once," they eventually feel overwhelmed and give in because they can no longer handle the pressure of living a different lifestyle from their family. Being overwhelmed by lifestyle changes comes from a place of not being convinced they are worth the effort or not really knowing why they want to be healthy.

However, when clients decide they must get their life back, no matter what, I could give them a hundred lifestyle changes and they would implement them all without question or hesitation. Many women think that getting healthy is a great idea. Unfortunately, they don't have the audacity to make it happen. They don't engage their wellness because they don't value their own life enough. Women have been taught to value pain and the identity it gives them more than the pleasure that living well will bring.

Be committed to seizing your wellness, no matter what.

Embracing Pleasure

Life comes with pain; however, we must allow ourselves to embrace pleasure so that we can truly feel alive. Part of feeling alive is to discover what brings us pleasure. When we have been disconnected from the pleasures of life due to overwhelming pain, it can be disheartening to realize that we have no clue what brings us joy anymore. Stuff doesn't bring us happiness; we experience fulfillment through the relationships and experiences we have along the way. This is especially true for the relationship we have with ourselves. We experience feelings of unfulfillment, unhappiness, and being unloved when we do not honor who we are, when we play the game of life as a pawn rather than the queen that we are.

Playing a role that is not true to who we are causes stress, anxiety, fear, and depression. We lose our radiance and feel pain and dissatisfaction with life, even though we seemingly have it all. Showing up as less than yourself doesn't work. We can fool people temporarily, but a woman who is paying attention always knows when she has let her crown fall to the ground. Sadly, so many women's crowns are on the ground covered in dirt. They no longer see themselves as valuable or worthy of love and pleasure. Even Cinderella pursued her dream of being the belle of the ball and marrying her Prince Charming. Why do so many women settle for living in a less than beautiful state and crush their own dreams? We can't expect to feel radiant and alive when we are playing small and ignoring who we were made to be.

We don't have to have the answers for our entire life. We are only promised today. Live well today to create your beautiful tomorrow. Asking myself daily questions helps keep me grounded and on track. *How do I want to show up today? How do I want to feel? What impact do I want to make in the world? What is holding me back today from living my most audacious life?*

Of all the questions, asking what holds you back is the most telling of all. The answer to this question, spoken from the depth of your soul, might startle or alarm you. When the unabridged version of you answers that question and you realize that what has been holding you back is yourself, it is unnerving. It is also why most women won't answer this question truthfully. As much as the truth hurts, it gives us insight into where we have been lying to ourselves. When we know the truth, we can stop sabotaging ourselves and our relationships and move forward living empowered, not blinded.

It's time to get real with yourself. Write down all the lies that you convinced yourself were true, that gave you the right to stay stuck in pain and misery, unable to move forward into your beautiful future. To engage with your life and embrace pleasure, you must destroy every lie, limiting belief, and soul-crushing story that you created out of these lies and replace them with the truth.

We Can Choose to Find the Silver Lining

In every story we can find a silver lining. Take my daughters' abuse, for example. I wasn't a bad mom. I did protect my girls. I did everything I could to ensure they were safe. There were bad players and situations that were out of my control. I couldn't control the wasp that stung my sister or the fact that she had an unknown life-threatening allergy. I couldn't control the actions of my brother. But I can control how I show up and how I continue to love despite the devastating rupture of my mama's heart. Just because I was emotionally devastated in the moment does not mean I was a lesser mother. That was a disempowering belief I told myself over and over. All I can control is my response to what is happening around me and within me. Unfortunately, my response at that time was to take all the blame of what had happened to my daughters and beat myself into a pulp. I made myself the villain in my story and labeled myself with that identity for years, adding fuel to my pain.

I locked down and became an even more intense helicopter parent so that this would never happen again. I trusted no one with my kids. I tried to control every aspect of my life and the lives of everyone around me. I became more rigid and more dysfunctional. I could not see beyond the pain. I could not see how changing the storyline could have helped us all to move forward faster and happier. I was stuck on my narrative of being the world's worst mom. This self-concocted story was destroying me, and I was taking everyone down with me.

The day I realized that this was just a nonsense story I had made up, I could finally see the silver lining in the circumstance. My daughters were safe, loved, and thriving. And out of the desperate cry of my mama's heart, I have a beautiful son whom I may have never met without this situation. Knowing deep down that I was an amazing mother was a true gift. The birth of my son was a blessing of a lifetime.

> *We get to choose the meaning of our life. We can—and we must—rewrite our story and create our own breathtaking ending.*

To fully engage and live an empowered life, we must annihilate the stories that are destroying us. Stop allowing yourself to be defined by the limiting beliefs and values you select out of your suffering and pain. We get to choose the meaning of our life. We can—and we must—rewrite our story and create our own breathtaking ending.

Life is too short to slump around disengaged, living as a shadow of who you were meant to be. Choosing to engage with your life despite the circumstances, diagnosis, or pain is the boldness that will allow you to thrive, not just survive. When you live out of audacity, you will find passion and pleasure once again. You are the queen of your vessel. You get to adorn it, beautify it, lavish praises on it, and express yourself through it. Audaciously set your ship sailing, choosing pleasure as your destination.

Lightbulb Moments to Build Audacity

1. Engaging and living life is more beautiful and fulfilling than hiding from it. Passionately show up in life as your authentic self.

2. Imagine what your life would feel like if you captivated, attracted, and fully occupied it.

3. The stories of our life can limit or enhance the definition of who we are and how we fit in the world. Be sure that the stories you are telling yourself are congruent with the woman you want to be.

Audacious Actions to Live Well on Purpose

1. What color would you be and why? How does that color make you feel? Does it enhance your mood? How do your thoughts change when you think about that color? Journal your thoughts and then buy or create something that color to remind you to show up for the day as the audacious and vibrant woman you are.

2. Picture what your life would be like if you were fully engaged in it, seeking pleasure and purpose out of a heart of pure love. Journal about what you will do differently to show up and engage your life to live well.

3. Tap into your pleasure center. Journal all the reasons why you are enough, and lavish truth praises on yourself, just like you would for your best friend.

CHAPTER 18

Having the Audacity to Live Well

I AM NOT living your life, nor do I know the hurts and pains or sufferings of your past.

We all have had horrible things happen to us along the way. Some of us have experienced a little more hell than others, but that's not the point. We cannot ever measure the challenges and circumstances of another's experiences against our own. We don't have the lens of their experience and the culmination of their trauma, perceived or lived.

Your past does not define you. The meaning that you give your traumatic and pleasurable events is what defines you and directs your life. Your historical events do not dictate your future but rather, how you saw those events and your role in them. Were you the victim, the heroine, the villain? Was the event a tragedy, a comedy, a drama, a love story, or a mystery?

How you choose to see your history sets up your future because your choices assume that your character can never change. If you see yourself as a victim, you are the victim in every story. In fact, you will design a horror show out of a romance to prove your character is always the victim.

Everyone with long-standing chronic disease has had as much turmoil as their body and soul could handle. The diagnosis was just the point that their body broke the emergency glass. Their mind and body started looking for an exit a long time before the alarm bell rang loud enough for a diagnosis to be made. They just ignored all the symptoms along the way. Some of us are too scared to go to the doctor to get a checkup, fearing the worst. But lack of early treatment can narrow the window of opportunity to help your body redirect course, and it can make the situation worse.

My body had been in constant pain for years. I had spent every day since Dr. Susan discharged me trying to find solutions to eliminate all pain from my body. Back pain was "normal" for me ever since the back injury I'd had when I was sixteen. It wasn't as if I didn't do anything to help myself. I did see a chiropractor regularly. Sadly, my healthy lifestyle did not go much beyond chiropractic care, gardening, and eating good old-fashioned, home-cooked meals. In the early days of the diagnosis, I didn't know there were other things I could have been doing to help my body become pain-free. I didn't even ask, and none of my doctors mentioned any other possibilities for treatment.

For many living with chronic pain, we tell ourselves it isn't really that bad, or that we should suck it up, or that others have more pain than we do. However, we can't compare our pain to anyone else's. Pain is entirely an individual perception based on our own history, circumstances, emotions, mood, and experiences. Do not wait to get help until it is so bad that you can't function. By then it is exponentially more challenging to treat. Find the support you need to feel good. If your doctor can't help you, find someone else. Ask at the health food store or the gym for referrals for alternative practitioners. Ask for support from friends who live a wellness lifestyle. They might have a yummy pain-killing smoothie recipe they can share. You can't get proper help from someone who doesn't understand what you are going through or have the experience to help you. Without health, you have nothing. Get help today and do not give up until you find something that works.

The biggest mistake in my journey was I didn't seek other help soon enough. I didn't research other treatments or strategies that I could have tried to help my body heal and recover from the initial back injury. I never considered talking to a professional about my stress, anxiety, or traumatic childhood events. Mental wellness was not "in" in those days. I was taught to suck it up and not to bring shame or embarrassment to myself or my family. Even after I was diagnosed, I was in so much pain that I could hardly move or do simple daily activities, and I lay in bed on my thirty-fifth birthday, seemingly living out the curse placed on me so many years before.

It took that cataclysmic disaster of a medication scandal to wake me up and decide to aggressively go after my health, to live well on purpose, no matter what it took and regardless of what it looked like.

Compared to everyone I knew, I lived a very healthy lifestyle. My husband and I didn't drink or smoke, we didn't eat out, and I grew a lot of our food. We were active in our day-to-day lives. But that wasn't enough. My body was missing key fuel sources such as proper sleep, decreased stress, and emotional wellness. My body was even rebelling at healthy foods such as potatoes, ancient grains, beans, and bananas, but I ate them anyway, not understanding the effects they were having on my body and the pain they were causing.

I don't have your diagnosis. I don't have your genetics. I don't know your lifestyle. But I do know that if you have chronic disease and pain, your body has run out of reserves to support, heal, repair, recover, regenerate, and recreate itself in a functional, life-giving way. It has run out of its innate ability to be *homeodynamic*, the ability to bring itself into balance regardless of the internal or external circumstances. If your body can't maintain life in a balanced way, it diverts critical energy to vital functions while the rest of the body is left to fend for itself.

I don't have your dreams, but I do know there is not one person alive who wishes to have a debilitating or life-threatening disease as one of their life goals. We avoid pain like the plague, doing anything we can to get away from it. That is why pain was and is used as a form of torture. Pain breaks us down mentally, emotionally, physically, and even spiritually as the anger, frustration, resentment, shame, bullying, and peer pressure silence our faith and put a wall up between us and God. How much pain will it take for you to draw the line in the sand and realize that you are not getting any better and that your prognosis is not on the side of living an abundant life and fulfilling your dreams?

Medication Versus Natural Solutions

People tell me that someone they know tried natural treatments and they died, using death as justification to prove that natural treatments don't work. Newsflash: millions of people try conventional medicine and put all their faith and trust in common medical treatments and still die. The only thing that both statements prove is our healthcare system is broken and people are dying.

If one hundred people take a medication and fifty die, and one hundred take a natural supplement and fifty die, the results are the same: fifty percent died regardless of the treatment. Yet we have been led to believe that natural treatments don't work and are a threat to life. Clinically, most people who used natural treatments during their illness had a higher quality of life, were happier, and had more meaningful family connection at the end of their life. We need to stop downplaying natural treatments. One is not better than another; they each have their merits.

After sixteen years serving my clients as a homeopath, holistic nutritionist, blood microscopist, and bioregulatory medicine practitioner, I have researched thousands of peer-reviewed papers on natural supplements and therapies as well as documented testimonies of recovery, remission, and cure. I have witnessed hundreds of seemingly incurable cases greatly improve or resolve completely using natural medicine and therapies. The efficacy of natural medicine has been supported using the same research methods as conventional medicine. Many natural medicines and therapies have been around for hundreds if not thousands of years, yet most of the medications in use today are less than twenty years old. Many of our most-used medications, such as aspirin and morphine, are derived from plants.

Conventional healthcare is not "health" care. It is a bandage that offers no real help because it doesn't get at the root of the issue, although it can be lifesaving in an emergency. Medicine uses descriptive words to describe your complaint, but it doesn't tell you why you have the problem. When you know the reason behind your health issue, you can address it and incorporate daily health habits that will help your body do what it was created to do: heal, repair, recover, restore, and regenerate itself, repeatedly. If your body is not doing those things, then you need to ask, "Why not?" and "What can I do to get back on track to live well every day?" Finding out the root cause of your health issues and giving the body what it needs to heal itself is where you will find true healing and vitality.

Many women say they are healthy, but when I probe a little deeper, they tell me about all the medications they are on. They say that the medications worked for them because their symptoms went away and they feel healthy. Health is not an absence of complaints. We measure our health on an ever-changing sliding scale according to how we feel, how long we have had symptoms, and how our symptoms compare to those around us. Let's take constipation as an example. Constipation may initially be annoying, but if it doesn't resolve, we become more concerned. Left untreated, constipation may become chronic. Because this is now our "new normal," we stop believing that we have a problem, because over time our definition of our bowel health has changed. Constipation is not normal and can contribute to other health issues, including increased pain, fatigue, indigestion, and headaches.

When women believe they are healthy because they are taking medication, I always ask what happens when they stop taking the medication. Inevitably, they say their the symptoms come back. The symptoms didn't come back—they never left. They were just being hidden by the medication. Symptoms, whether hidden or experienced, are not a state of health. This is a limiting belief that gives you permission to continue living the lifestyle you always have lived, expecting your body to spontaneously heal itself even though you have done nothing to improve your health. When you stop a medication and all the symptoms come back, or when you must keep taking medication to avoid feeling symptoms, then that medication is not working. It is not healing you; it is placating you, trying to convince your mind that nothing is wrong. If it were working, you would be healed.

Wearing a bandage and pretending you didn't cut your finger off doesn't make your finger whole. You need to get the end of your finger sewn back on to fix your problem. A bandage won't fix your finger; it just gives the illusion that it does by covering the real issue, your missing fingertip.

Medications used for chronic and autoimmune diseases are bandages. The disease continues to progress and eventually becomes a larger issue, causing greater suffering. Sometimes we take other medications to cover up the side effects of the original medication. We don't need more medication; we need to fix the root cause.

We rely on medications for three reasons. One reason is because we are told there is no hope of reversing autoimmune disease. Sadly, this is true, because most of us are not willing to do what it takes to help our body heal itself. We are content to take medication to mask our pain rather than investigate the root cause and use natural solutions to help

We don't see healing very often because we do not seek to be healed. We just want to escape the pain.

the body heal. The second reason is that we no longer believe our body is capable of healing itself, so we don't even try. I challenge that thought process and say we don't see healing very often because we do not seek to be healed. We just want to escape the pain. Thirdly, we don't know what we don't know. I am not against medicine or needed surgery, but they should not be our primary solution. For example, a headache is often a sign of dehydration. When some people have a headache, they drink a large glass of water, and their headache goes away. Others take a pill to mask the pain, but it doesn't solve the dehydration problem.

We must do more than take medications to achieve optimal wellness. There is no quick fix. Wellness is a lifelong journey, not a moment in time. Your body is missing vital ingredients to heal. This is the realm of natural solutions and a wellness lifestyle. These ingredients are simple, but they are not easy to incorporate for many busy women.

The Missing Ingredients

Food

Food is not like medicine—it *is* medicine. Nutritious, unprocessed, naturally occurring foods of all the colors of the rainbow should be your dietary focus. Eating a diet that is as close as possible to the way the food is grown and with as little preservation or cooking as necessary is the ideal for your body to be able to maximize digestion and absorption of the nutrients that it needs to perform optimally.

Water

Drink water. If it isn't water, it's not water. Do not be fooled by the false information that anything that you drink is basically water and hydrating. Only water is water. Milk is food; it is protein and fat. Soda is sugar. Teas and coffees are diuretics and flush water from the body. Juice is also similar to food because it is filled with sugars and other nutrients. Most women are chronically dehydrated due to lack of water in their diet. Dehydration contributes significantly to various symptoms, aches, and pains in the body as well as increased aging. We feel better, more energized, and sharper when we are adequately hydrated. Drinking half of your body weight in ounces per day is a good rule of thumb for proper hydration and for helping your body eliminate toxins and waste. Water is a natural energizer. Wash away fatigue by drinking more water.

Reducing Stress

Reduce your stress levels. Stress is a killer. It is a killer of mood, energy, relationships, digestion, and elimination. Stress sabotages our hormones and blood sugars, elevates our blood pressure, ruins our sleep, and just generally makes us feel crappy. Do something that you truly enjoy every week, something that makes your heart sing and your spirit soar; I call this rejuvenating rest. These types of activities fuel us, feed us, and restore our soul. These hobbies also help lower our stress levels. Hint: if your hobby or activity is competitive and gets you all riled up, it is not restorative; it defeats the purpose. The activity can be highly physical, but if it creates stress and tension because you must win, this is not the hobby that will help you decrease your stress level. Many women are so out of touch with what they love to do because they have spent years putting themselves on the back burner. These women may have to try a variety of activities or hobbies before they find one that truly fills them up. That is perfectly okay; it is all a part of the adventure.

Sleep

Getting proper sleep is crucial to our health. Adults need seven to nine hours of sleep every night. Your body has a lot to do when you sleep. The sleep we get before midnight is restorative. The sleep we get after midnight is when our body is regenerating, healing, detoxing, and recovering itself. Waking throughout the night can reveal which organs or systems in your body are struggling to heal, repair, and regenerate. It is not normal to wake up at night, especially at the same time every night. For example, waking every night around 3:00 a.m. suggests that your liver is having problems detoxifying. Drinking celery juice or dandelion tea daily may help resolve this issue.

Similarly, your body has been designed to concentrate its urine so you can sleep through the night. If you urinate frequently throughout the night, applying juniper berry essential oil over your bladder and kidneys may provide support to your urinary system and help you sleep better. If you keep waking during the night, work with a natural healthcare practitioner who looks at the root cause rather than someone who just prescribes a medication to knock you out.

Recreation

Recreation is all about getting out there, moving your body, and having fun. When we move our body, we enhance our mood because of the release of those feel-good hormones called *endorphins*. It's not as much about a specific type of exercise as much as it is about having fun, breathing, and moving your body in a way that feels good. It's a win-win situation.

> *Too many women work out because they hate themselves, not because they love themselves.*

I was the queen of stiffness, rigidity, and pain. Regardless, I got up and showed up every day. I went to the barn and tended to my animals, gardened, cleaned my home, and made love to my Mr. Wonderful.

Movement creates flow in your life. Without movement we become stagnant and inflexible. It is crucial to move your body as much as you can every day. The more you move your body, the more relaxed it will become and the more movement it will tolerate. But when you don't move, you lose your ability to move.

Move your body as a sign of love, not of hate. Too many women work out because they hate themselves, not because they love themselves. There is a huge difference between the two. One woman works out to punish her body, while another works out to love her body back to life. Go for quality of life. Incorporate loving movement into your day to live life to its fullest.

Reducing Toxicity

Reducing your toxic load, physically and emotionally, can help alleviate many symptoms. Toxins are pervasive in the world we live in. From radiation, chemicals, cleaning products, body care products, and even our food, we are bombarded every day by chemicals that are toxic to our cells. We don't have to wonder why our health disintegrates so rapidly. Coupled with the reality that most people do not fully eliminate their own waste daily through proper bowel movements, the accumulated toxic load in the body exponentially increases, causing the body to slow down and become sluggish in its function. Toxicity affects every cell and organ system in our body, causing increased fatigue, brain fog, lack of energy, moodiness, digestive and neurological disturbances, aches, pains, and more. Sometimes we don't need medication; we need to detoxify and clean out our body.

Reducing your exposure to toxins is just as important as proper daily elimination. The easiest way to reduce toxic exposure is to use safe, natural cleaners for your body and your home.

Relationships

Our relationships should be life-giving. We can't dismiss how integral nurturing relationships are to our well-being, both physically and emotionally. We must be in loving, nurturing, supporting relationships and community. Women need community. Women are hardwired to be in a supportive tribe with other women of all ages to learn, grow, and support each other. Women do not do well disconnected from authentic, loving relationships.

Relationships require two people. They should not be

one-sided or parasitic, sucking the life out of you every time you get together. You should not always be the giver or the receiver. Every relationship should be essentially equal. There may be times when you give more or receive more from the other, but overall things should flow in an even exchange, where you both feel valued and respected.

Consistency

Although these lifestyle habits may seem overly simplistic, they are not easier than popping a pill. Lifestyle habits demand consistency. Your body does not easily forget the abuse that it suffered. For example, if you have been chronically dehydrated, you may have to drink sixty-four ounces of water every day for months before your body starts absorbing it. We underestimate the immense

Part-time health habits do not create health.

healing power that a consistently healthy lifestyle can give us. Drinking water may not help us to feel better instantly, but over time as the body rehydrates itself, every cell comes alive and we'll see our pain and inflammation decrease. Living healthy 50 percent of the time will not increase your health by 50 percent. In fact, you won't see much improvement at all. Wellness is a long-term relationship, not a one-night stand.

Part-time health habits do not create health. Most people do not continue with a wellness lifestyle because they want instant results with little effort. When we don't get instant results, we try the next thing that comes our way. If you put gas in your car 50 percent of the time, and the rest of the time you fill the gas tank with cola, it wouldn't take long before your car refuses to take you anywhere. The same is true with your body. Your body is very resilient and can withstand a lot of abuse. But when we abuse ourselves daily, over years, the scale starts to tip, and the body can no longer function properly. This dysfunction causes pain and disease.

Health Poverty Is One of the Greatest Epidemics in Our Society Today

The peer pressure from our friends, family, and social media to eat, drink, overschedule, self-sabotage, and exhaust our bodies and minds influences us to fit in and be liked by everyone else. We are health poor, and it's an epidemic. Everyone around us is unhealthy or has chronic disease, and because it is so common, we think these issues are normal. Arthritis, diabetes, and heartburn are not normal. We live in the slums of health. We have health poverty and don't realize it. Women are pressured to conform and be like those around them—to eat the same, abuse their bodies the same, take the same medications, and think the same negative thoughts about themselves. We have created and encouraged health poverty, just to be like everyone else.

When we allow others to live our life for us, or when we allow peer pressure to design and sculpt our life, our thoughts, and our level of health, we have stopped listening to what our own body, soul, and spirit need. When we allow someone who hasn't figured it out for themselves to speak into our life and create course corrections that go against who we are and what we want, we are dishonoring our innate wisdom, dreams, and desires for our health and life.

For example, if I wanted to lose thirty pounds in six months and keep it off, would I ask my BFF who has been on a yo-yo diet for the past twenty-five years for their expertise, or an anorexic twenty-year-old social media influencer who has never had a weight challenge their entire life? No, because their life experience does not measure up to what I need at this moment in my life. I would want to find a wellness coach who has successfully helped women in my age group with my autoimmune issues or metabolic issues successfully lose weight safely and naturally.

Most people who have not struggled with a particular health or life challenge can't really help us because our problem-solving toolboxes are generally built on past experiences and continue to develop as our experiences and the way we see them are challenged.

If you have never broken a bone in your body, it is impossible to know how it would feel. Regardless of all the descriptive words, grunts, groans, and facial expressions that people who have broken bones use to explain the pain to us, we simply have no frame of reference for that kind of pain. We can only assume what it would feel like.

However, if you had broken your arm and your friend calls to tell you that they just broke theirs, you know what it feels like.

You might even give tips to them to help with the pain, swelling, itchiness, or burning sensations as they are healing because you know what they might experience as they heal.

We can explain how we feel and our experience of the event; however, the meaning we give to the language we choose is often not the same meaning that those around us have. Your husband will describe your birthing experience very differently than you because his experience was different than yours. What he saw, felt, and heard was different than what you experienced.

Tell a Better Story

The meanings we choose to give our life's experiences, and how we describe them, either drive us forward or slap us back. Hearing the stories of other women who have gone through similar experiences and thrived can help us reframe our stories and reimagine them, creating better outcomes and new endings. Use the experiences of other women to lift you up and propel you out of your pain.

Most women I have met are secretly lonely, sad, discouraged, depressed, frustrated, or unhappy. They put on a good show with a beautiful smile and singsong voice, but they are miserable and unfulfilled. Refuse to be held hostage any longer by the stories you are telling yourself about why you can't be healthy. Refuse to live your life by substandard definitions of health. Stop masquerading around as someone else. Wear your own crown.

Be audacious. Choose to believe that your life is good, and live out of that belief. Your story will be transformed and you will start experiencing life on a whole other level. You will see beauty all around you, hear sounds of joy, touch the passion of romance, smell the fragrance of pleasure, and taste that life is truly good.

An audacious wellness lifestyle empowers women to stand up for themselves and their bodies, to take bold risks that allow them to live fully alive, to love themselves so deeply that they can set themselves free from all their pain, and to love with passion and purpose.

Everything you need is already inside you. You were made to shine. Decide how boldly you want to show up and the kind of woman you want to be. I am a fearless lioness, a brave queen, a daring goddess, a courageous warrior. Who are you? Be the audacious woman you were born to be.

If you have gotten offtrack and have downgraded yourself from queen to housekeeper or heroine to victim, close your eyes and breathe the smells, see the sights, dream the dreams, feel the wind blowing in your hair, and call yourself back to the woman you know you are. Plot the course to the destination of your dreams, put on those stilettos and your finest lingerie, and make your move into a life of passion, fulfillment, and joy. Create your life authentically and make it beautiful, just like you.

When the road bumps come, and they will, roar like the audacious warrior you are and stand firm in your power as the queen of your life. Be unwavering in your new truths about who you are and who you are not. Stay committed to your new wellness lifestyle. Living well is beyond the realm of medicine. This is the realm of a wellness warrior—a woman brave enough to believe that it is possible to live well; to regain, restore, repair, and reinvent herself outside of a diagnosis; and to engage her wellness and create her own beautiful life, a life worth living and fighting for.

You've totally got this. You are an audacious wellness warrior.

Lightbulb Moments to Build Audacity

1. Don't wait for your Prince Charming to sweep you off your feet to feel loved. Start accepting and loving yourself right now. When we love ourselves and our life, we radiate, and that feels amazing.

2. Don't wait for the next best medicine. Act now. Be the change you want to see. Make the changes that are needed to live life more fully, starting now.

3. A wellness lifestyle is simple, not easy. Love yourself enough that you choose to make the best choices for your health.

Audacious Actions to Live Well on Purpose

1. What is something you are proud of in your life? Go back

to that time. Close your eyes and experience it all over again in Technicolor. Feel all the feelings, hear all the excitement. Live your amazing accomplishment all over again. Journal this experience so that you never forget how awesome you are.

2. What ingredient of a wellness lifestyle are you missing the most? Make a plan to incorporate this lifestyle habit into your daily routine. First decide the outcome, what you want to get out of this lifestyle change. Then write down all the reasons why you must add this lifestyle habit into your life. Once you have decided on the outcome and the why, the how will be much easier to attain. For example, I want to eat grain-free because I don't want to feel awful anymore. I don't want to feel bloated because it makes me feel gross, my clothes don't fit, my stomach gets hard and painful, and all I want to do is sleep. I will go through my pantry and collect all the grain-based products and donate them to a food bank. I will go online and find highly recommended cookbooks for grain-free living. I will take a cooking class for grain-free breakfast ideas. You've totally got this!

3. Choose the type of woman you want to be. Are you a warrior, a goddess, a queen, a lioness, a mother, a maiden, a healer, or a lover? How do you want to feel throughout your day? How do you want others to feel when they are around you? Write down the qualities and characteristics that you want to live your life by.

CHAPTER 19

I Am Blessed: Next Steps to Audacious Wellness

I AM BLESSED beyond measure. I have white diamonds, blue diamonds, and black diamonds. I have opals, onyx, and emeralds. I have sapphires and garnets. I have tanzanite and pearls. My Mr. Wonderful has blessed me with earthly treasures that are beautiful to behold. I am blessed indeed. But of all the treasures I can see and touch, the greatest treasure that I have is an amazing husband who loves me and has encouraged me to love myself—a husband who constantly reminds me of who I am even when I refuse to see it or forget altogether, who loves to see my smile and the joy in my eyes, who delights in seeing me come alive in the fullness of my radiance.

Of all the riches that I possess, the greatest is the audacity to live my life well and not take *no* for an answer. The backbone of that is my faith in Jesus.

As my faith in Jesus grew, it became an audacious tenacity to live my life, not just survive, because I understood what Jesus had done for me at the whipping post and on the cross. My faith that I was healed gave me the boldness to get back up regardless of the wave that tried to crush me. My faith taught me to ride the waves and master the winds as I rode. I learned to ride on top of the problem rather than be swallowed up by it, simply by changing my perspective and focus. I learned to find the blessings in the moment to find hope and joy despite my circumstances. The choices that I made in faith with the audacity of my actions shifted my life 180 degrees.

Choices Create Your Road Map

The first audacious choice I made was to choose life over a diagnosis. Because of that one choice, an avalanche of bold choices and positive results happened. I consistently choose peace over fear, health over medication, and pleasure over pain. I choose to tap into and stand firm in the power of the woman that God created me to be.

I make the choice to be a generous giver, a passionate lover, and a radiant soul. I choose to see how life is happening for me, not to me. And I make better choices about how I show up in the world around me.

I also choose language that lifts me up rather than beats me up. I choose meanings for my challenges that help me see the silver lining so I can thrive in any circumstance, undaunted and fearless. Part of choosing more empowering language is asking better questions such as, *How can I be and live even more passionately in this moment?* or, *How can I increase my energy right now?*

I used to ask questions such as, *What did I do wrong?* or, *Why me?* That type of questioning never gets us anywhere. It causes us to presume there is something wrong with us, and the focus becomes what is wrong, not what is right. There can never be a good solution when I direct the question in a blameful way

> *Questions that start with **how** help us find our solution.*

at myself. Telling myself what is wrong with me won't fix the current situation. It doesn't help us look for a way to correct the problem or move forward. Questions that start with *how* help us find our solution. *How can I add value to this situation? How can I show up as my best self right now? How can I choose to love myself in this moment? How can I move my body to feel more alive right now?* How-based questions direct us toward empowering action steps to find resolve and do our best given the situation rather than hurting ourselves even more. Asking how-centered questions demands that we look at the blessings in the situation or the blessing we can be to the problem. Changing the question changes the story and prevents us from focusing on pain and suffering rather than pleasure and love.

Life is a blessing for those who choose to see it that way, or it can be a curse with no hope in sight for those who are running away from it. It is all about the choices you make.

My purpose for sharing my story is not to tell you how to live but to convince you that you can, to inspire you to believe there is more for you than the life you are currently experiencing. Perhaps your life is already outstanding, and you are living the life of your dreams. That's fantastic, and I would encourage you to dream even bigger, because we never fully arrive. Our destination goalposts should be constantly moving with each step forward that we take. If you are not yet living the life of your dreams, look at whether you are progressing forward, giving freely, expressing gratitude, or being spontaneous.

Progress

Happiness in life comes from progress, not achievement. Achievement gets boring after a while. If we have no goals or dreams and there is nothing left to achieve, it is documented that our quality of life and perception of happiness start to decrease exponentially. Regardless of their diagnosis, the happiest people are the ones who are always working on improving themselves, their health, and their relationships. They are also the ones who are giving and contributing to the world around them and finding joy in the giving to help others move forward as well.

Giving

Giving brings us joy. If you feel like there is something missing in your life, and you have great relationships with yourself and others, try volunteering at a charity that you are passionate about. It is a fantastic way to give more of yourself and serve those in need out of love and passion rather than obligation. Giving allows us to see that we can bless others out of the abundance of blessings in our own life.

Dreaming bigger is not about getting more jewels, shoes, or a bigger home. It is also not about success, fame, or fortune. These things will never give you true pleasure or stop your pain. The happiness that these things may bring us is superficial and fleeting. We can feel fulfilled only when we are overflowing with happiness, love, and gratitude from within and giving freely of ourselves to the world around us. Happiness is a state of being, not an action. Happiness is not attained by what someone does but by our internal mood, spirit, and state of being.

Gratitude

Gratitude is an expression of appreciation for life itself. Of course, we can feel grateful that we have a good job or that our bills are paid or that we received a gorgeous new diamond necklace. But gratitude comes from acknowledging that you are alive and that life itself is good. We are grateful for our job because it means we are healthy and can work. We are grateful for the necklace because it means someone loves us very much. Gratitude is about acknowledging that we are alive, engaging with life and the experiences that being fully alive gives us.

Gratitude is about acknowledging the blessings you have been given and being thankful for them. I am full of gratitude for my life—the good, the bad, and the ugly—because the challenges and trials prove that I am alive. Without challenges or problems, we die. We cannot survive if we are not pressed at some level. All of creation must go through pressure in order to survive. A caterpillar must struggle out of the chrysalis to become a butterfly. If we try to help it, it will die. Babies must learn how to latch on to the breast and suckle or they will fail to thrive. Struggle is a part of life. No parent watches their baby fall when trying to take a step and says, "I guess you weren't made for walking. You should give up." No, we encourage them, we cheer them on, and we call out the walker in them. And so it should be for every area of our lives. Challenges give you the opportunity to move forward, try something new, and get out of the stagnancy of an unlived life.

Spontaneity

I am blessed to have lived a life of many trials and struggles. Without the pain, the pleasure would not seem as sweet. We can get comfortable and lazy in the status quo. We can wander aimlessly through life, missing the beauty in our stupor of normalcy. Routine is good to give structure to our day, but when we rely on structure to survive, any bumps along the way can set us off and cripple our day, week, month, or life. Spontaneity and adventure are good for the soul. They allow us to blossom, grow, and experience a bit more of the world around us in fascinating and exciting ways.

I didn't always believe this. My old story of pain and suffering told me that spontaneity and adventure were scary and something to be feared because I couldn't control what was happening. Spontaneity made me feel like I was out of control, and I resisted it with everything I had. When I rewrote my story and chose living life over controlling life, I had to come to terms with the fact that I was not in control, and I never was. This was a major shock to my system. I didn't want to believe that I could not be in control, because the story I had accepted said that if I wasn't in control, I wasn't safe.

When I discovered that safety was never certain regardless of how much I planned or tried to control situations, that truth bomb ruptured my heart and soul. At that moment, I had to decide what my truth was going to be. Would I continue to believe the lie and try to pretend that I was in control? Or would I trust that God was in control and that He is for me not against me, that His plans toward me are for good?

As I obsessed over these questions, I started to have flashbacks of all the times my safety had been threatened. I saw the entire event of the flasher in the woods at the elementary school, the call to the police, and the lineup of scary-looking men whom I had to identify at the police station.

I remembered the man who pulled up beside me as I was walking to work, grabbed me, and tried to pull me into his car. I was saved by a guy from school who just happened to come around the corner at the right time.

I recalled the time when I was getting into my car with my six-month-old baby at noon in the parking lot of our apartment complex, when two men tried to get into the car with us.

And I remembered the night I had closed the restaurant and my parents couldn't come to pick me up. There were two men in a pickup truck who had been in the restaurant earlier who had told me they would be waiting for me after my shift. I was afraid to walk the one and a half miles home because something didn't seem right about these two men. After multiple calls home, and still not finding anyone available to come and pick me up, I finally decided that I was being ridiculous, and I was fine. I locked up and started walking as quickly as I could, hoping they wouldn't notice me. They saw me right away and started honking and catcalling me. They started their truck and began following me. I started to panic and walked faster. I didn't want to look afraid, but it was nearly midnight, the roads were empty, and there was no one in sight. When I crossed the intersection there was some traffic, and the men were held up, so I took off my slip-on shoes and ran like hell. I ran so fast I thought my legs would fall off. My heart was beating out of my chest and the men were gaining on me. So I did the only thing that I could think of: I ran into someone's backyard and hid in their bushes. The men got out and followed me into the backyard. They looked around for me for what seemed like an eternity. I was frozen in fear. I was so afraid to go back to the road that I jumped four blocks of fences through people's backyards to get home to safety.

As I reflected on these incidents, I realized that God was in control, that He saved me and protected me. God shielded me from harm over and over again. He was my safe refuge and place of safety, and I could access Him anywhere. I didn't need to micromanage my life anymore. I was free to create my own beautiful life.

I was blessed; I just didn't see it at the time. I had stopped living because I had been frozen in fear. The stories we tell ourselves about what happened in our life can propel us toward our destiny or cause us to hide in fear. Stories can limit us or cause us to grow. They can cause us to act in irrational ways or become better versions of ourselves. Stories can change the entire trajectory of our life and our ability to give and receive pleasure. The narrative that runs in our mind can have us focusing on fear and pain and cause us to shelter in place, not wanting to live our lives.

I wish I had known these things when I was younger. I

would have told the story with me as the warrior heroine rather than the victim. I wonder what my life would have been like if I had lived as the heroine of my own story. It's hard to assess that, but I know I missed out on a lot of opportunities due to fear, pain, and my need for control.

We can't go back and change our experiences or delete the memories from our mind, but we can rewrite the stories in more powerful ways, turning them into a life-giving tales with victorious endings that will change the road map of our life forever.

> *Life is happening for me, not to me.*

Rewriting my story has totally changed my life. My outlook is positive; life is happening for me, not to me. I have come to love a good adventure, and I show up as my true self everywhere I go. I am not a victim. I am a warrior, a heroine, a goddess, and a queen.

I am the audacious wellness warrior. I have grabbed my life by the horns, and I will ride it all the way to the end full of passion, with love, audacity, and joy as my weapons and dance as my rear guard. I want to lay it all down and leave nothing on the table. I want to exhaust every ounce of love and passion that I was given and pour it out on the world.

Abundant Life

God's promise is life, and that more abundantly (John 10:10). My audacity to live well was birthed out of a choice to be free from pain and to feel more pleasure by living my life, not merely trying to survive it. I wasn't living the abundant life that God promised. I was living as a prisoner in my own body and mind, living a life I had created out of the pain and suffering I was focused on. I wanted more, I needed more, I deserved more, and I was going to get my life back, whatever it took.

There is no way in hell I would ever get in that wheelchair—not then, not now, not ever. I choose abundant life, and you can too. If you have been doing the audacious actions at the end of each chapter, you are well on your way to living a life of abundance.

To live an abundant life, you must define what that means to you. Take time to answer the following questions:

1. What do you need to say *no* to so that you can live more abundantly?

2. In what area(s) of your life do you need to be more alive?

3. Create your definition of health and ask yourself why it is important to you. When you have the answer, ask yourself again why that's important to you. Write down your answer and ask the question again. Repeat the process five times to really push yourself for the truth of why your health is important to you. You must know why health is important to you and why you want to be healthy so that you can make bold choices and take consistent actions to see your dreams fulfilled. What you think health is today may change next year.

4. Create your wellness support team by partnering with healthcare practitioners who align with your wellness goals and will empower and encourage you to live well. If you are not seeing improvements despite incorporating all their recommendations, find another practitioner. If you have only been picking and choosing the wellness habits you want to incorporate, try consistently doing all of their recommendations for optimal progress. Remember, health is not a part-time pursuit.

Simple Steps to Live Audaciously Alive

1. Drink plenty of water: half your body weight in ounces every day.

2. Remove all sugar, processed foods, and caffeine from your diet. Pro tip for even faster results: eat grain-free for ninety days; this includes no rice, corn, or their derivatives.

3. Eat a large salad every day.

4. Eat the colors of the rainbow.

5. Feed your soul by doing something that brings you pleasure for fifteen minutes every day.

6. Get eight hours of sleep every night.

7. Pray or meditate daily, breathing deeply to help release any tension.

8. Move your body for thirty minutes a day.

This is not a dress rehearsal. Show up for your life. You are enough. You deserve it. Start living well today. May my story inspire you to love yourself enough to be boldly audacious, find the warrior within and create your own beautiful life.

Lightbulb Moments to Build Audacity

1. Blessings can be found in every moment if look for them.

2. Rewrite your story in a way that helps you see you've thrived in life's challenges; you were not a victim to them. You are an overcomer, a warrior, a queen.

3. Gratitude is about being thankful for your life. When we are full of gratitude, we live a richer, more vibrant, fulfilled life.

Audacious Actions to Live Well on Purpose

1. Keep a daily gratitude journal. Every day write three things for which you are truly thankful and why. What we focus on grows. If we focus on the blessings of life, we will see more to be grateful for.

2. What is your greatest treasure? What is your greatest possession? What makes each special to you? How can they serve you to show up more authentically in life?

3. What is one question you can ask yourself to help you find a better solution for your current health challenges? Hint: start your question with "How can I . . ."

"Unstoppable, she is a perpetual force, like time she moves forward despite everything." —J. Iron Word

May you forever be
audaciously alive!

Acknowledgments

FIRST, I WOULD like to thank Scott McKain for mentoring me and encouraging me to write my story of healing so that women can be healed and set free from their chronic pain and diagnosis and their spouses can understand how best to support them as they continue to love each other through the pain. Thank you for sharing your story with me. You are a true inspiration.

Thank you to Jonathan Merkh and Forefront Books for the amazing opportunity to tell my story to help women suffering with chronic disease find their way to healing. Jennifer Gingerich and the editing team, you are fantastic. I am grateful for your grace and believing in my ability to cut 30,000 words! Thank you to the graphic design team for getting the shoes just right. You totally rock!

To His Excellency, Dennis Ignatius, former High Commissioner of Malaysia to Canada, and his beautiful bride, Cherry, thank you is not enough to express my gratitude for sharing your love and passion of Jesus and His healing power with me. Your love and friendship over all these years have been a blessing. I have been inspired and moved by your unshakeable faith. You both mean so much to me. Without that touch from Jesus so many years ago, I may have never truly known how high, how wide, or how deep His love for me is. Many years ago, you told me to write my story. Here it is.

To Dr. David, without your patience and commitment to help me live and move pain-free, I am not sure I could have survived. Your dedication, house calls, and emergency appointments do not go unnoticed. Thank you to your bride, Katrina, for putting family plans on hold so you could get me out of pain and back on my feet. Thank you for always knowing that living pain-free was possible, that God is a God of miracles, and for endlessly adjusting my neck from writing this book!

To Faisal Naqvi, thank you for not capping my dreams and for encouraging me to dream bigger. Thank you for believing in the impossible and never allowing me to give up. Thank you for not just pushing the limits but believing with me that there are none because our bodies are wonderfully created by God. Thank you for helping me get out of my own way and be fully me. Thank you for being a sounding board and calling me higher as I relived the pain while writing this masterpiece.

To my children, Ashleigh, Hannah, Cadence, and Johnathon, I live for you. You are my treasures, my pride and joy. Thank you for your understanding as I wrote this book and missed dinners and get-togethers when I was stuck in my office. Thank you for loving me despite the grumpy moods, and for your patience when I couldn't walk as fast as you or do the things that you wanted to. We always found a way to live life well. My desire is that you will always choose to make the best choices and live audaciously alive every day.

To Scott, my Mr. Wonderful—Babe, it hasn't been easy, but we did it together. Thank you for pushing me and not